Praise for
The Chickpea Revolution Cookbook

"If you thought chickpeas were boring, be prepared to be stunned. As a fellow chickpea enthusiast, I can relate to the love for the mighty bean, however, I am still wowed by the creativity, deliciousness, and beautiful photos in this book! The variety of things you can do with chickpeas will have you wanting more!"
—Sophia DeSantis, author of *Vegan Burgers and Burritos* and founder of the blog *Veggies Don't Bite*

"I love this book! Looking to the chickpea is an easy, healthy, delicious step all of us can take to reduce our carbon footprint. Mitigating climate change is complex. It takes more than Tesla and wind turbines. It requires a cultural shift in everything we do and how we do it—especially deciding what we eat."
—Wesley Normington, executive director TREC Education and climate reality leader

"Heather Lawless and Jen Mulqueen show world-class versatility of the humble, healthy chickpea. From a clever, impossibly crunchy granola to a playful, decadent poutine, I was amazed at just how many ways you can add chickpeas, in all of their forms, to everyday meals. "
—Allison Day, author of *Whole Bowls* and *Purely Pumpkin* and founder of the blog *YummyBeet*

"A pile of chickpeas is more than just a hill of beans in the hands of Heather Lawless and Jen Mulqueen. Not all superheros wear capes; these revolutionaries don aprons on a mission to save the world, one legume at a time. Their creative recipes will empower the everyday citizen to take a stand against climate change by simply eating more plant-based meals, without sacrificing time, taste, or money. Environmental activism has never been so delicious."
—Hannah Kaminsky, author of *Real Food, Really Fast* and BitterSweetBlog.com

"As the author of the cookbook *Aquafaba*, I am supremely aware of the importance, benefits, and possibilities of chickpeas. Heather and Jen (and I) want everyone to get on board the Chickpea Revolution and make the future a brighter, happier, more empathetic, and more delicious world for all generations of today and tomorrow."

—Zsu Dever, author of *Everyday Vegan Eats, Vegan Bowls*, and *Aquafaba*

"Versatile and highly nutritious, the chickpea offers great health benefits. Rising food prices, and the modern day epidemic of obesity, diabetes and heart disease make the chickpea an alluring choice. Furthermore, the many positive environmental effects of eating a plant-based diet offer an additional incentive to move in this direction and live more sustainably."

—Dr. Eileen Nicolle, family physician

"Chickpeas pack incredible punch when it comes to fiber, protein and some key vitamins and minerals. Raised on an Indian vegetarian diet, the chickpea was a staple in our pantry. *The Chickpea Revolution Cookbook* has opened my eyes to just how versatile the chickpea can be in so many other types of cuisine. This cookbook will revolutionize your life through a healthy diet and the joy of cooking!"

—Dr. Meeta Patel, emergency physician, assistant professor,
faculty of Medicine, University of Toronto

"Forget everything you thought you knew about the chickpea. Authors Lawless and Mulqueen have launched the unassuming garbanzo into legendary legume status. From falafel dogs and sushi to pakoras and crème brûlèe, their beautifully photographed recipes demonstrate just how much we've underestimated the culinary capacity of the chi chi bean. So grab your kitchen utensils and get ready to join the revolution."

—Sandra Sellani, coauthor of *The 40-Year-Old Vegan*

THE CHICKPEA REVOLUTION COOKBOOK

THE CHICKPEA REVOLUTION

COOKBOOK

85 Plant-Based Recipes for a Healthier Planet and a Healthier You

HEATHER LAWLESS and JEN MULQUEEN

Skyhorse Publishing

Skyhorse Publishing books may be purchased in bulk at special discounts for sales promotion, corporate gifts, fund-raising, or educational purposes. Special editions can also be created to specifications. For details, contact the Special Sales Department, Skyhorse Publishing, 307 West 36th Street, 11th Floor, New York, NY 10018 or info@skyhorsepublishing.com.

Skyhorse® and Skyhorse Publishing® are registered trademarks of Skyhorse Publishing, Inc.®, a Delaware corporation.

Visit our website at www.skyhorsepublishing.com.

10 9 8 7 6 5 4 3 2 1

Library of Congress Cataloging-in-Publication Data is available on file.

Cover design by Jenny Zemanek
Cover photo credit Josh Neubauer

Print ISBN: 978-1-5107-2640-6
Ebook ISBN: 978-1-5107-2641-3

Printed in China

Dedications

Heather
To GG, for teaching me that cooking and singing go together like a wink and a smile. To M, for continuing to make my life "overwhelming good." To e & j, for always giving me something to fight for.

Jen
To Mike, for continuing to believe that you got the better end of the deal, when I'm clearly the winner. To Audrey & Hazel, for making the world a better place . . . and for eating so many chickpeas.

Chickpea Pot Pies

Contents

Introduction

Worried about being held responsible for the destruction of the planet? What if you learned that one small thing—eating more plants and plant-based foods, including chickpeas—could lead to a healthier planet and a healthier you? Come join the revolution!

As you're likely aware, climate change is the most pressing environmental issue we've ever faced as a civilization. Significant impacts are being felt around the world due to rising sea levels and extreme weather events. Greenhouse gas emissions from human activity, including raising animals for food, are driving climate change.[1] In fact, the United Nations has described the livestock sector as "one of the most significant contributors to the most serious environmental problems, at every scale from local to global."[2] Even more tragic, the effects are being shouldered by the world's poorest and most vulnerable. [3]

Animal agriculture accounts for 18 percent of all greenhouse gas emissions,[4] more than the exhaust from all cars, planes, trains, and ships combined![5] Eco-anxiety (yes, a real thing) is on the rise, and many of us are living with chronic worry that if we don't act now, it will be too late. The good news is that activism can help counter these feelings of helplessness, and we need all hands on deck to fight for a healthier planet!

In the big picture, policy changes, international cooperation, and the structural transformation of our economy will be critical to control runaway climate change . . . but these changes will be expensive and take years to implement. Urgent action is needed now, and we want you to join in! Most people are unaware of how impactful eating less meat can be for addressing climate change. A global shift to consuming less meat could result in a quarter of the emission reductions needed to keep the world below the dangerous level of 35.6°F (2°C) warming.[6]

Eating more plant-based foods is a delicious form of activism that will make you happier, healthier, and, in the long-run, feeling confident in knowing that you were part of the revolution that led to a more sustainable planet. You can start making a difference now with that patient can of chickpeas waiting in your pantry to be consumed. When wielded effectively, that can of chickpeas will help to revolutionize your kitchen. *The Chickpea Revolution Cookbook* will give you fresh takes on old favorites, new ways of composing meals, and the tools you need to incorporate more plant-based foods into your diet. We have your back when it comes to transforming what was once a meat dish into a Mother Nature–loving meal.

So, why did we write this book?

As parents of young kids, we've been struck with the immense responsibility of raising caring and engaged humans. We are committed to handing down a world that's in better shape than it is today, and we firmly believe that incorporating more plant-based meals into diets will improve the world. We also love great food!

We've both worked with *Roots of Empathy*, a school program that helps raise children's social and emotional competencies and increase their capacity for empathy. Striving to be kind and respectful to other humans offers a natural segue toward being kind and respectful to animals and the planet. This book offers recipes that, for us, are an extension of the principles we share in the classroom.

The Chickpea Revolution Cookbook is all about:

- Finding fresh, local, and organic ingredients where possible
- Frequent high fives
- Ensuring everyone gets enough to eat
- Messy kitchens
- Small changes that can add up to make a big difference
- Well-loved kitchen tools
- Cooking with kids
- Sustainable agriculture
- Experimenting with food
- Not taking ourselves too seriously

- Informal food gatherings
- Respecting cultural differences
- A great playlist while we cook
- Viewing food as a powerful tool to bring about positive change

Why all the hype about chickpeas?

Don't get us wrong—we love all kinds of legumes. Eating more beans and veggies in general, especially as a substitute for animal products, is a climate-saving victory. However, chickpeas have a special place in our hearts because of these revolutionary qualities:

1. *They're versatile.* As you'll see in this book, the chickpea is *crazy* versatile. The humble chickpea has seven thousand years of culinary prowess under its belt. No other bean, or food for that matter, can perform the shape-shifting tricks of the chickpea. You can eat it raw, roasted, deep fried, blended, mashed, sautéed, or whipped into a froth. Chickpeas are used in a vast array of cuisines around the globe, which you'll see represented in this book (Indian, Spanish, Syrian, Thai, Italian, Mexican, Canadian, New Zealand, and more).

2. *They're environmental crusaders.* Chickpeas are mini environmental warriors! These beans are "soil builders" due to their ability to absorb atmospheric nitrogen as a source of nutrients, rather than relying on fertilizer, which can degrade soil quality over time.[7] By contrast, crop production for animal consumption is heavily reliant on fertilizers and a very inefficient use of arable land. It is estimated that livestock production accounts for 70 percent of all agricultural land use and occupies 30 percent of the land surface of the planet.[8] Our reliance on animal products is also accelerating climate change through deforestation, and it has destroyed approximately 90 percent of the Amazon Rainforest.[9] Chickpeas have no need for grazing, nor do they flatulate and belch methane (cows emit this gas, which is twenty-five

times more powerful than carbon dioxide!).[10] While some might argue that the bean could give you gas, no human body could match the climate-warming power of a cow.

3. *Chickpeas are the bean of the future.* Chickpeas are getting ready for climate change. Major research is being done using wild chickpeas and sequencing genotypes to create a better bean that can be resilient in the face of extreme weather like drought, flooding, and frost.[11] For example, the International Crops Research Institute for the Semi-Arid Tropics has sequenced more than 90 chickpea genotypes with 28,000 genes and several million genetic markers hoping to develop superior varieties.[12] Further, USAID (United States Agency for International Development) and the University of California Davis launched the five-year Feed the Future Innovation Lab for Climate Resilient Chickpeas.[13] This bean has our back when it comes to feeding the future.

4. *Chickpeas fight for food security.* Every day, close to 800 million people go hungry. What's maddening is that the world's livestock are fed enough grain to feed 3.5 billion people![14] If we make changes to our way of eating, we can help ensure that food is more equitably distributed. Chickpeas are affordable, versatile, and rich in protein. They have the capacity to play an important role in the world's looming food crisis. Every day, researchers are working to improve the bean's protein, iron, and zinc content.[15] In the past ten years, new breeds have increased chickpea-growing areas six-fold with production increasing from 95,000 to 884,000 metric tons per year worldwide.[16] New strains of chickpeas are able to grow in areas that previously could not support the crop and strains that can produce in shorter growing seasons. This means that what was once a subsistence crop is now a significant income generator and export commodity for small farmers that need it the most.

5. *Chickpeas are good for you!* Unless you're living under a rock, you've no doubt heard that eating too much red meat (especially processed meats) can increase your risk of cancer and heart disease. Industrialized countries are eating on average twice as much meat as is considered

healthy.[17] Unfortunately, meat-industry groups continue to go to great lengths to dissuade policy change from happening,[18] but a recent study found that if people lowered the amount of meat they eat to a more modest amount, more than five million deaths could be averted over the next thirty years.[19] This figure rises if more people were to adopt a plant-based diet.[20] Chickpeas are a great source of protein, fiber, iron, phosphate, calcium, magnesium, zinc, and vitamin K. Countries around the world, including Netherlands, the United Kingdom, and Brazil, are stepping up to promote the health and environmental benefits of eating less meat. After extensive public consultations, Canada's next iteration of the Canada Food Guide is expected to eliminate dairy as a food group and promote more plant-based options as the preferred source of protein. It's about time the chickpea gets the attention it deserves!

So how can you use chickpeas?

Great question! What makes chickpeas so magical is their versatility. Some say they are like the unicorn of beans (okay, maybe that's just us). Chickpeas come in many shapes and sizes and in a multitude of forms. Though the most common type of chickpea appears round and beige, other varieties can be black, green, and red. Here's an overview of how we've used chickpeas in this book:

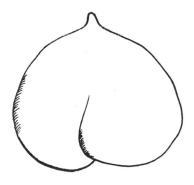

Dried Chickpeas: Dried chickpeas, also known as "desi" or "kabuli," come in a variety of shapes, sizes, and colors. Black chickpeas, for example, are perfect for darker dishes, like Chocolate Chickpea Brownies (page 149) or to add an aesthetic color contrast to a dish. Cooking dried chickpeas is by far the healthiest and cheapest way of preparing them. Cooked chickpeas freeze really well so you can make a large batch and always have them on hand. See page 157 for instructions on cooking a perfect batch of chickpeas.

 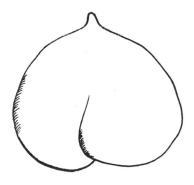

Canned Chickpeas: Canned chickpeas have the benefit of being incredibly convenient. If you've got a can opener, you're in the club. They also offer instant access to aquafaba, the liquid that beans are stored in. There are a couple things to be mindful 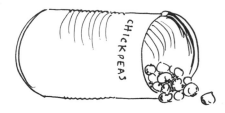 of when purchasing canned garbanzos. Sodium: low or no sodium beans are becoming more readily available in supermarkets, but if the can you've purchased contains high amounts of salt, be sure to rinse and drain them before using to remove up to half the sodium. It's also important to be aware of Bisphenol A (or "BPA"), an industrial chemical that has been used to make certain plastics and resins since the 1960s and has toxic implications on ecosystems. Exposure to BPA is a concern because of possible health effects of BPA on the brain, behavior, and the prostate gland of fetuses, infants, and children. Many brands, such as Amy's and Eden Organic, sell products in BPA-free packaging.

Chickpea Flour: Chickpea flour, also known as "besan" or "gram," has some incredible properties. It's gluten-free, high in protein, and very inexpensive. In this book, it's found in all forms of baking, frying, and many types of pasta. The one thing that we struggle with is its taste before it's cooked. It's got a very strong flavor that some may find off-putting. Essentially, it means you can't lick the bowl of the cookies, brownies, or muffins that you're making. But if patience is your strong suit, this  is the flour for you! If you're in a bind, or just in a pioneer mood, you can blend dried chickpeas in a powerful blender. Send the flour through a fine sieve to remove any lumps.

Aquafaba: Aquafaba (Aqua = water; faba = bean) is the common name of the liquid that beans are stored in or the liquid that remains when you cook your own. It was just discovered in 2015 and has revolutionized vegan cooking. Its most astounding property is as a replacement for egg whites due to its ability to emulsify, foam, bind, and thicken. You'll find aquafaba is used widely in this cookbook (New Zealand Pavlova, Lemon Meringue Pie, Pasta Fagioli with Sneaky Chickpeas, cocktails, Mayonnaise), but the limits are endless. Something that used to be thrown away can now be used to make

incredible food. Once again, chickpeas are lookin' out for the planet. For instructions on how to make your own, please see page 165 in our Tips, Hacks & Libations section. Adding cream of tartar to the aquafaba helps to create stiffer peaks faster. It's possible to make a frothy whip without this addition, but including it is a real time saver.

Chickpea Pasta: Chickpea pasta is turning up in health food stores across the world. It's super high in protein and fiber, and other nutrients such as thiamine, magnesium, iron, and antioxidants. It's also gluten-free and vegan. There are several brands we enjoy, including Chickapea, Maria's Healthy Noodles, and Banza, but check your local supermarket or natural health-food store for options in your neighborhood.

A Note on Organization

People often ask us if we're sick of chickpeas, and our answer is always a resounding *no!* The humble chickpea is so versatile that we never tire of finding new and exciting ways to incorporate it into our dishes. It's time everyone started including this superstar food in their culinary creations.

We want our plant-based recipes to be simple to make, affordable, and delicious. While vegan foods tend to be healthier, don't expect this book to serve up your average "health food" offerings. We're all about comfort foods that happen to be healthy and great for the planet.

The Chickpea Revolution Cookbook is organized into eight chapters that fit your busy lifestyle, giving you more time to fight the good fight. Our breakfast chapter helps you get your day off on the right foot with recipes such as savory Breakfast Burritos (page 11) and Morning Glory Muffins (page 9). Our appetizer chapter helps you and your guests to get into the party mood, with quick and easy Socca Bread (page 30) and crowd-pleasing Buffalo Cauliflower-Pretzel Wings (page 33). The food truck chapter includes the stuff you wish you'd see more of when you're on the go (and hopefully will in the future!) including Fish-less Tacos (page 46) and a Falafel Dog (page 45).

As we move further into the book, our easy weeknight chapter offers you recipes that can be whipped up in a flash if you're coming home late from the office or dashing off to your enviro book club. Recipes include Soba Noodles with Chickpeas and Ginger-Miso Dressing (page 67) and our vegan chickpea version of a Sloppy Joe, the Garbanzo Joe (page 63). We've also included a chapter that's not only perfect for smaller kitchens with limited space but the featured dishes also make cleanup a breeze. One-pot favorites include our Rockin' Moroccan Stew (page 87) and Spanish Style Chickpeas and Spinach (page 83).

When you want to impress a crowd, our entertaining chapter offers you stunning dishes such as Acorn Squash Salad with Black Chickpeas, Roasted Grapes and Lemon-Tahini Dressing (page 120), and Chickpea Pot Pie (page 106). And don't forget our dessert chapter, which showcases the chickpea prowess as a star when it comes to finishing a meal. Everyone will be thrilled when you throw down recipes such as Crème Brûlée (page 128) and Double Chocolate Chickpea Cupcakes (page 146).

Finally, we finish with a chapter outlining kitchen tips and hacks, as well as a few cocktail recipes that feature chickpeas. You deserve a cocktail after all your hard work making the world a better place.

Fight for the Bean!

The *Chickpea Revolution Cookbook* arms you with more than 85 recipes that help you incorporate more plant-based and sustainable foods into your diet, including chickpeas. These recipes will score you high fives from Mother Nature, will have you eating hearty and nutritious meals, and will have your friends scrambling for a dinner invite. Advocacy is more important than ever, and *The Chickpea Revolution Cookbook* helps you address the most pressing environmental challenge humanity has ever faced. Be sure to get your hands dirty and have fun!

CHAPTER 1
Wakey, Wakey, Earth Ranger

Start-the-Day-Off-Right Granola

(Serves 4)

Eating this granola for breakfast is like filling up your tank with premium gas.
But wait—gas isn't good for the environment, and definitely not a good thing to eat
for breakfast. This granola is a much better idea. The chickpea flour helps everything
clump together in delicious, satisfying nuggets. Combine with some vegan yogurt or
almond milk and show the day who's boss!

Ingredients

3 cups old-fashioned oats
½ cup walnuts, chopped
½ cup pecans, chopped
½ cup almonds, whole
½ cup sunflower seeds
½ cup pepitas
½ cup chickpea flour
½ cup coconut oil, melted
¼ cup maple syrup
½ tsp salt
1 tsp vanilla
1 tbsp cinnamon
½ cup dried fruit (i.e., raisins,
    apricots, dates)
2 tbsp hemp hearts

Directions

1. Preheat oven to 350°F.

2. In a large bowl, combine oats, walnuts, pecans, almonds, sunflower seeds, pepitas, and chickpea flour.

3. In a smaller bowl, combine coconut oil, maple syrup, salt, and vanilla. Pour the wet ingredients into the dry and stir until completely mixed. Pour mixture onto greased cookie sheet and sprinkle cinnamon on top. Cook for 40 minutes. Try not to stir it if you want a chunkier consistency. Remove from oven and allow to cool.

4. Once cooled, add dried fruit and hemp hearts.

Yamcakes

(makes 10 pancakes)

This recipe is so good that people will invite you to their cottages, country homes, and [insert place you want to go] just so you'll make them Yamcakes. Jen's husband is the mastermind behind these unique pancakes, and she will happily have him make them for you at your vacation home in exchange for an invite. Just say the word. These Yamcakes will also serve you well as a breakfast in bed item if you're trying to impress someone. Pair with Chickpea Breakfast Sausages (page 6) and Maple Baked Beans (page 7) for a breakfast homerun.

Ingredients

2 tbsp ground flax
3 tbsp warm water
1½ cups shredded yam (about 1 medium yam)
1 tbsp coconut oil
1 medium onion, thinly sliced
1 tbsp organic brown sugar
½ cup chickpea flour
½ cup all-purpose flour
½ cup coconut sugar
½ cup quick-cooking oats
1 tsp baking soda
½ tsp salt
¼ tsp cinnamon
¼ tsp curry powder
½ cup walnuts, finely chopped
2 cups of your favorite non-dairy milk such as almond, cashew, coconut, or soy milk

Directions

1. Place flax in warm water and let sit for 10 minutes.

2. Set a pot of water to boil and add shredded yam. Allow to boil for 3 to 4 minutes. Drain and set aside.

3. In a skillet, melt coconut oil on medium heat and add onions and brown sugar. Let cook, stirring occasionally for 20 minutes until caramelized. Be sure to scrape up the sweet bits on the bottom of the skillet as you go.

4. In a large bowl, combine the chickpea flour, all-purpose flour, sugar, oats, baking soda, salt, cinnamon, curry powder, and walnuts.

5. To the large bowl, add milk, flax mixture, cooked yams, and caramelized onion, and stir until combined.

6. Pour ¼ cup of the batter onto oiled skillet. Cook each side for 2 to 3 minutes until golden brown. Serve with maple syrup.

Yamcakes, Chickpea Breakfast Sausages (page 6), and Maple Baked Beans (page 7)

Chickpea Breakfast Sausages

(Serves 12)

Vegan sausages are the perfect savory sidekick to any breakfast. They also pack a protein punch, so they're great for lunchboxes, too. Serve alongside Yamcakes (page 4), Maple Baked Beans (page 7), fresh fruit, or toast with smashed avocado and you've got yourself a breakfast of champions! Xanthan Gum may sound like a scary ingredient, but it's actually just a thickening agent produced by fermenting sugars. Still sounds scary? Feel free to leave it out but be extra gentle when frying the sausages as they may be more inclined to crumble or fall apart.

Ingredients

1 cup crumbled tempeh
½ cup chickpeas, canned or cooked
¼ cup white onion, diced
2 cloves garlic, minced
1 tsp jalapeno pepper, minced
1 tsp organic brown sugar
1 tsp smoked sea salt
1 tsp fresh ground black pepper
¼ cup nutritional yeast
1 tsp xanthan gum
1½ tsp fennel, crushed
1½ tsp smoked paprika
2 tbsp fresh parsley, chopped
2 tbsp soy sauce
1 tbsp olive oil

Directions

1. Add all ingredients except olive oil to a food processor. Pulse until well combined. Remove and shape into mini sausages, approximately 3 inches long and ½ inch in diameter.

2. Wrap each sausage in a small piece of foil. Steam for 10 to 15 minutes (we use the steamer on our rice cooker, but you can use a pot steamer as well). Place in fridge for 1 to 2 hours or up to 24 hours.

3. When ready to eat, heat olive oil in a skillet. Working in batches, fry each sausage for 3 to 5 minutes, turning often until golden brown all sides. Serve immediately.

Maple Baked Beans

(Serves 4–6)

Who doesn't love baked beans at brunch? Even people who typically don't like beans have a fondness for this sweet and savory breakfast sidekick. Usually baked beans are made with navy beans, but chickpeas can easily play the role, and you're more likely to find a can or two in your pantry. Best part is that this recipe only takes an hour to cook, meaning you can sleep in longer!

Ingredients

3 cups cooked or canned chickpeas
½ cup aquafaba (reserved from cooking dried beans or from a can of chickpeas)
1 cup of your favourite marinara sauce
2 tbsp molasses
½ tbsp sea salt
2 tbsp yellow mustard
¼ cup maple syrup
1 onion, very finely diced

Directions

1. Preheat oven to 400°F.
2. In a casserole dish, combine chickpeas, aquafaba, marinara sauce, molasses, salt, mustard, and maple syrup.
3. Add onion on top of beans (this will help them cook faster).
4. Bake for 1 hour. Check the beans after 30 minutes. Once the onions have started to brown, stir them into the dish with the rest of the ingredients.

Morning Glory Muffins

(Makes 1 dozen regular-sized muffins or 8 jumbo muffins)

We heart everything about these muffins! The fact that they have carrots in them practically means they're a salad. These somehow top Heather's dad's list of the favorite foods, and he normally doesn't go for cooked veggies. They're lovely warm out of the oven, but also great the next day for lunch boxes or a snack. Add a dollop of vegan margarine if you're feeling decadent.

Ingredients

1 cup medjool dates
2 tbsp ground flax
4 tbsp warm water, divided
1 tsp vanilla extract
½ cup organic brown cane
    sugar
1 cup almond milk
½ cup coconut oil
1 tsp fresh ginger, grated
1 cup chickpea flour
1¼ cups all-purpose flour
1 tsp salt
2½ tsp baking soda
1 tsp cinnamon, ground
¼ cup raisins
¼ cup sunflower seeds
    (optional)
1 cup carrot, grated
1 cup apple, peeled and
    grated

Directions

1. Preheat oven to 350°F.
2. Place dates in a bowl and cover with boiling water. Let sit for 20 minutes. Drain, saving ⅓ cup liquid.
3. Combine 1 tablespoon flax with 3 tablespoons water. Let sit for 10 minutes until thick.
4. Place dates in a food processor with vanilla and reserve liquid and process until smooth. Transfer to a bowl and add sugar, almond milk, oil, flax mixture, and ginger.
5. In separate bowl, whisk together flours, salt, baking soda, and cinnamon. Combine the wet and dry ingredients and mix in raisins, seeds, carrots, and apple.
6. Pour into a greased muffin tin. Bake for 22 to 25 minutes, or until a toothpick comes out clean.

Maple Cinnamon Overnight Oats

(Serves 4)

Despite this dish being insanely easy and quick to whip up, you'll feel like a domestic goddess/god pulling it out of the fridge in the morning. In one fell swoop, the masses will be fed a delicious, protein-packed, nutrient-dense meal. Top with fresh berries, nuts, or warm non-dairy milk. This dish also travels well and is perfect for a mid-morning snack. It's delicious served cold but feel free to warm up if you prefer.

Ingredients

2 cups quick-cooking oats
1½ cups non-dairy milk, such
   as soy, almond, or cashew
½ cup chickpeas, roughly
   chopped
1 very ripe banana, mashed
2 tbsp maple syrup
1 tbsp cinnamon
1 tsp sesame seeds
Fruit, nuts, or additional seeds
   (optional)

Directions

1. In a dish with lid, combine oats, milk, chickpeas, banana, maple syrup, and cinnamon. Sprinkle with sesame seeds and cover. Place in fridge overnight.

2. In the morning, scoop into serving bowls and top with any additional toppings you wish, such as fruit, nuts, or extra seeds.

Breakfast Burritos

(Makes 10–12 small burritos)

These delectable burritos are a staple at Jen's house. She makes them in advance and has them ready for a brunch or a weekend away. They're also perfect to drop off for friends who've just have just had a baby. Seriously, what new parent won't love a healthy and delicious "one-handed power burrito"? If you choose to make a whole bunch and freeze or give away, do so after Step 5 below.

Ingredients

1½ cups yams, peeled and diced into ½-inch cubes (about 1 medium yam)
1½ cups cooked or canned chickpeas
1 cup aquafaba
1 clove garlic, minced
½ tsp cumin
½ tsp smoked paprika
½ tsp sea salt
½ tsp pepper
1 tsp olive oil
¼ cup pepitas
2–3 green onions, chopped
½ cup salsa
1 package small tortillas
1 whole avocado, sliced

Directions

1. Heat oven to 350°F and roast yams on an oiled baking sheet for approximately 20 minutes, or until soft.

2. Meanwhile, add the chickpeas and aquafaba to a blender, along with garlic, cumin, paprika, salt, and pepper. Blend until smooth.

3. Warm olive oil in a skillet over medium heat and pour chickpea mixture into the pan. Stir often, allowing mixture to reduce and brown, for about 5 minutes.

4. Set up an assembly line of roasted yams, pepitas, green onions, salsa, and the chickpea mixture.

5. Lay tortilla flat, spread chickpea mixture on top, and add all ingredients, being careful not to overfill. Fold sides inwards and roll into tight burrito.

6. Return to oven and bake for 15 minutes or until the tortilla is crispy.

7. Serve with avocado and condiments of your choice. Or just eat as fast as possible while jiggling a new baby.

Zucchini, Walnut & Fresh Herb Fritters

(makes 8–10 fritters)

There are times of the year when we're zucchini rich! They grow so abundantly in warm weather that people are giving them away with a look of panic on their faces. This is the perfect recipe to break out in those moments. Or at any moment when you want to eat something crispy, full of flavor, and overflowing with vegetables and protein. These fritters are great at brunch and also work well on the go as a snack. Walnuts give it a great crunch. No eggs are needed with these fritters because the chickpea flour is a wonderful binder. Take these fritters to the next level by serving with the tahini dressing.

Ingredients

2 medium zucchinis (yields about 3 cups grated)
1 cup chickpea flour
1 tsp sea salt
4 tbsp olive oil, divided
1 onion, chopped
2 cloves garlic, minced
3 tbsp fresh herbs (rosemary, chives, parsley, whatever you have on hand), chopped
⅓ cup walnuts, chopped

For the dressing

¼ cup tahini
½ lemon, juiced
1 tbsp olive oil
1 tbsp soy sauce or tamari
1 clove garlic, finely chopped
¼ tsp salt
1 tbsp chives or parsley, chopped
2 tbsp warm water

Directions

1. Grate zucchini and remove excess water by placing in a clean dish towel and squeezing out as much water as possible.

2. Place grated zucchini in large bowl and add flour and salt. Set aside.

3. Warm 2 tablespoons of olive oil in skillet on medium heat. Cook onion for about 4 to 5 minutes, until soft. Add garlic, and cook for an additional 1 to 2 minutes. Add to bowl with zucchini.

4. Add chopped herbs and walnuts and combine well.

5. Heat remaining 2 tablespoons olive oil in skillet. Pour zucchini mixture into skillet in ½-cup portions. Cook for 3 to 5 minutes, or until golden brown. Flip and repeat on other side.

6. Meanwhile, make tahini dressing by combining all dressing ingredients in a glass jar with a lid and shake well. Serve with fritters.

Banana Chocolate Chip Oatmeal

(serves 2)

This amped-up weekend breakfast will get your kids eating their oats. The chopped chickpeas mimic the texture and consistency of the steel-cut oats, so no one will know that pulses have found their way into this breakfast favorite. But the extra protein will put a spring in your step and keep you fueled until lunchtime.

Ingredients

3 cups water
1 cup steel-cut oats
½ cup canned or cooked chickpeas, chopped into tiny pieces
½ cup non-dairy milk
1 very ripe banana, mashed
1 tbsp shredded coconut
1 tbsp chia seeds
1 tsp cinnamon
⅓ cup vegan chocolate chips

Directions

1. Place water in a large pot and bring to a boil. Add oats, reduce heat, and cook for 10 to 15 minutes.

2. Stir in chickpeas, milk, banana, coconut, chia seeds, and cinnamon. Cook for 2 to 3 more minutes.

3. Sprinkle with chocolate chips and serve.

CHAPTER 2
Let's Get This Party Started

Sweet Potato Chickpea Sliders with Carrot Slaw

(Makes 10–12 sliders)

There's something inherently adorable about sliders. Maybe it's their cute little buns or mini garnishes. All we know is that when we bust these out at a party, everyone wants in. They also happen to be a hit with little kids, who have a hard time committing to a full burger (every host has cringed at the abandoned one-bite-n-done burg). If you're super organized and want to prep in advance, feel free to cook a batch of these and pop into the freezer until you're ready to rock and roll.

Ingredients

For the burgers

2 tbsp flax
1 cup, plus 3 tbsp water
2 large sweet potatoes or yams, peeled and cut into 1-cm cubes (yields about 3 cups)
3 tbsp olive oil, divided
½ cup quinoa
2 cloves garlic, minced
½ small white onion, diced
1 cup chickpeas, canned or cooked
¼ cup fresh basil, chopped
½ tsp spanish paprika
1½ tsp sea salt
½ tsp fresh ground pepper
10–12 small slider buns or dinner rolls
½ cup arugula

For the carrot slaw

2½ cups carrot, grated
4 tbsp vegan mayonnaise, store-bought, or homemade (see page 158)
1 tsp dijon mustard
1 tsp apple cider vinegar
1 tsp fresh parsley, chopped
Juice from ½ lemon
Fresh ground pepper, to taste

Directions

1. In a small bowl, whisk ground flax with 3 tablespoons water and set aside.
2. Set a large pot of water to boil. Add sweet potato, reduce heat, and simmer for 10 to 12 minutes until potatoes are tender. Drain and set aside.
3. Boil 1 cup of water and add quinoa. Reduce heat and simmer for 10 minutes until all water is absorbed. Remove from heat and fluff with a fork. Set aside.
4. Mash chickpeas with a fork or potato masher.
5. Heat 1 tablespoon olive oil on medium heat and sauté garlic and onions for 5 minutes. Remove from pan and place in a large bowl. Into the same bowl add chickpeas, sweet potato, quinoa, flax mixture, basil, garlic, and onion. Shape into small patties and place on a baking sheet. Place in freezer for 10 minutes (this step helps them stay together when cooking).
6. In a skillet, warm remaining olive oil on medium heat. Working in batches, cook burgers for 3 to 5 minutes until browned, then flip and cook on other side for 3 to 5 minutes.
7. In a small bowl, mix all ingredients for carrot slaw until well combined.
8. Place sliders on small buns and top with carrot slaw and a few sprigs of arugula.

Classic Hummus

(Makes approximately 2 cups)

This hummus is exceptional, if we do say so ourselves. In fact, after trying out this recipe, our friends from Syria told us this hummus tastes like "home." We prefer to use dried, soaked, and cooked chickpeas (page 157), but canned chickpeas also work well. Serve with warm pita bread, cut veggies, or schmear onto a sandwich with some sprouts and tomato slices. However you choose to serve this hummus, we're sure you'll be making it often.

Ingredients

1½ cups cooked or canned chickpeas
⅓ cup fresh lemon juice (approximately 2 small lemons)
1 cup tahini
1 cup cold water
½ cup olive oil, plus more for drizzling
3 cloves garlic, finely minced
1½ tsp sea salt
½ tsp cumin
Pinch of paprika, for garnish (optional)
1 tbsp olive oil, for garnish
Fresh ground pepper, for garnish

Directions

1. Add all ingredients to a high-speed blender and blend for 2 to 3 minutes until very creamy, stopping to scrape down sides and adding more water if necessary.

2. Place in a serving dish and sprinkle with paprika, a drizzle of olive oil, and fresh ground pepper.

Chickpea Polenta Crisps with Olive Tapenade

(Makes about 18–20 crisps)

These fancy-pants appetizers are great for when your boss is coming over for Happy Hour. The crisps take a bit of pre-planning, as the chickpea tofu needs to sit for a couple of hours. But the tapenade is a breeze to whip up, so you'll make up for lost time. Keep this recipe in mind when you're looking for ways to use up your chickpea tofu as the recipe makes an impressive amount and you'd be deeply saddened if it went to waste.

Ingredients

1 batch Chickpea Tofu (see page 155)
½ tsp coarse sea salt
¼ cup green olives, pitted and chopped
½ cup black olives, pitted and chopped
¼ cup chickpeas, chopped
1 tbsp olive oil
⅛ tsp dried rosemary, crushed
½ cup fresh basil leaves (the tiny leaves from the center of the plant are ideal but you can also slice the leaves into small strips)

Directions

1. Preheat oven to 425°F.
2. Slice chickpea tofu into long, thin slices (about ¼ of an inch). Using a small circle cookie cutter (a shot glass also works well), create small circle shapes and carefully pop out. You may wish to use the sharp point of a knife to help with this.
3. Place on a parchment-lined baking sheet and bake for about 10 minutes and then flip. Cook for 5 more minutes or until golden brown. Remove from oven and allow to cool.
4. Make the tapenade by placing sea salt, olives, chickpeas, olive oil, and rosemary in a food processor and pulsing until well combined but still chunky.
5. Place a dollop of the tapenade on each polenta bite and place a small basil leaf on top.

Breadsticks

(Makes 10 breadsticks)

Great for kids and grown-ups alike, these handheld snacks offer minimal mess and maximum nutrition. So if your kids are inclined to protest against eating anything that isn't beige, serve them these. Because, protein. They're great on their own as a munchie, but pretty enough to offer guests whose bellies are rumbling as they wait for the main course. We've offered three sprinkle options below—feel free to use one or all three if you're feeling artsy. Pair with our Classic Hummus (page 19), your favorite dips, or throw down some Marinated Chickpeas (page 158) if you're building an appie platter.

Ingredients

2 cups chickpea flour
½ tsp salt
½ tsp baking soda
½ tsp pepper
3 tbsp olive oil + more for painting on breadsticks after baking
8 tbsp water
1 tbsp sesame seeds (optional)
1 tbsp poppy seeds (optional)
1 tbsp Chickpea Parmesan (optional, see page 159)

Directions

1. Preheat oven to 450°F. Line baking sheet with parchment paper.
2. In a large bowl, combine flour, salt, baking soda, and pepper. Add olive oil and 7 tablespoons of water. Knead dough until pliable, adding remaining tablespoon of water if required.
3. Divide dough into 10 balls and roll into an 8-inch rope. Or if you want a twisted breadstick, divide the 10 balls in two and twist 2-inch ropes together.
4. Place on the baking sheet and paint or rub with olive oil. If desired, sprinkle with sesame, poppy seeds, or vegan Parmesan.
5. Bake the breadsticks for 15 minutes or until golden brown. Serve warm or cool.

Hot Spinach, Artichoke & Kale Dip

(Serves 6)

This is a favorite of ours because we love cheese and we love hot. This dip can be whipped up in a flash and never fails to impress friends and loved ones. If you're going mobile with this dish, save the baking part until you've arrived, as it's best served piping hot out of the oven (also, carrying a hot dish through a crowd yelling, "coming through!" is great way to break the ice at a party). We like to serve this dip with Fritos—they go together like a wink and a smile—but feel free to use tortilla chips, warm pita, or anything else that begs to be dipped.

Ingredients

½ cup cashews
½ cup white carrots, chopped
¾ cup cauliflower, chopped
¾ cup potato, peeled and
    chopped
½ cup cooked or canned
    chickpeas
3 tbsp nutritional yeast
1½ tsp sea salt
1 tbsp fresh lemon juice
½ tsp garlic powder
½ tsp onion powder
⅓ cup olive oil
1 cup warm water
3 packed cups baby spinach,
    chopped
1 cup marinated artichoke
    (from a jar or can), chopped
1 cup green kale, chopped
½ cup swiss chard, chopped

Directions

1. Preheat oven to 425°F.
2. Place cashews in a bowl and cover completely with warm water. Allow to sit for 20 minutes.
3. Set a medium pot of water to boil. Add carrots, cauliflower, and potato, reduce heat, and cook for 10 to 12 minutes until vegetables are soft.
4. In a high-speed blender, combine cashews, vegetables, chickpeas, nutritional yeast, salt, lemon juice, garlic and onion powders, and oil. Start to combine and slowly add warm water. Blend until smooth and creamy.
5. Place greens and artichoke in a baking dish and pour "cheese" over top, stirring to combine. Bake for 20 minutes until top is golden brown and bubbly.

Stuffed Grape Leaves

(Serves 8)

With the guidance of a close family friend from Syria, Heather created the delectable chickpea version of this Middle Eastern staple, also known as *yalanji*. It's the kind of recipe that's simple but time-consuming, so clear your schedule for the morning. Bonus: Wrapping and rolling the *yalanji* is actually fun and even a bit meditative. We recommend a strong coffee and a little Sunday morning jazz before you get to work. Note: This recipe calls for pomegranate molasses, which can be found in a Middle Eastern supermarket or specialty food store.

Ingredients

500g jar of vine leaves packed
   in water
1 cup olive oil
1 large onion, diced
2 cups white medium-grain rice
1 tbsp tomato paste
3 tbsp red pepper paste
1 cup cooked or canned
   chickpeas
Juice from 2 lemons
   (about ⅓ cup)
2 tsp salt
1 tbsp pomegranate molasses
4 medium tomatoes, diced
1 packed cup parsley, chopped
½ cup mint, chopped
2 potatoes, sliced (or steaming
   rack for bottom of pot)
Freshly ground pepper, to taste
Lemon wedges, for garnish

Directions

1. Place vine leaves in a colander and rinse well. Set aside.

2. Warm oil on medium heat in a large pot. Add onion and cook for 4 to 5 minutes until translucent. Add rice and stir to coat. Turn heat down to low. Add tomato paste, red pepper paste, chickpeas, lemon juice, salt, and pomegranate molasses. Cook on low for 20 minutes, stirring occasionally. Remove from heat, stir in tomatoes, parsley, and mint, and set aside.

3. Boil a large pot of water and place the vine leaves in the water for about 2 minutes to remove excess salt and brine. Place in a colander, rinse again, and set aside to drain.

4. Open the vine leaves on a cutting board one at a time, with the smoother side down. Put 1 tablespoon of the mixture horizontally on each, fold in 2 sides, then roll tightly into a small cylinder shape (similar to a small cigar).

5. Place steaming rack or sliced potatoes at the bottom of a large pot. Tightly pack

the stuffed leaves on the potatoes or rack. Add enough water so grape leaves are completely covered with water. Place a ceramic plate on top of the leaves with a heavy can or jar on top of it (this prevents the leaves from opening or floating around). Bring to a boil and immediately reduce heat to low. Cook for 1 hour.

6. Drain excess water, allow to cool, and then arrange on a serving plate. Serve at room temperature with lemon wedges. Note: The potatoes are tasty, too!

Crispy Lettuce Wraps

(Serves 4)

This dish is based on one of our favorites from a vegan restaurant that's taking Toronto by storm. It's light and decadent at the same time, and the DIY toppings make it a fun and interactive dish to serve to guests at a dinner party. Oyster mushrooms have a hearty, satisfying texture. Once fried, the crispy mushrooms pair well with the refreshing lettuce. Use vegan "fish" sauce, and lime juice to create the sauce—and hot peppers (called *phrik nam pla* in Thai) are an irresistible addition if you're cool with a bit of heat.

Ingredients

1 cup vermicelli noodles
½ tsp each of dried rosemary, oregano, and thyme
1 batch Perfect Batter (page 156)
1 pint oyster mushrooms (approximately 2 cups), broken into bite-sized pieces
Oil, for frying
2 tbsp soy sauce
1 tsp sesame oil
½ cup vegan fish sauce (or soy sauce)
1 tbsp fresh lime juice
2 hot Thai chilies, minced
12 small lettuce cups or leaves from a head of iceburg lettuce
1 cup sliced multicolored mini peppers
1 tsp sesame seeds
Baby beet greens or other colorful baby green, for garnish

Directions

1. Set a small pot of water to boil. Add vermicelli noodles and cook for 3 to 5 minutes. Drain and set aside.

2. Mix herbs into batter.

3. Warm 1 to 2 inches of oil in a deep pan on medium-high heat. Working in batches, dip the mushrooms in batter, and then place in the oil. Fry for 4 to 5 minutes, turning halfway, until golden brown. Remove and place on a paper towel–lined plate to absorb excess oil.

4. In a medium mixing bowl, combine rice noodles, soy sauce, and sesame oil.

5. Make the dipping sauce by combining vegan fish sauce, lime juice, and hot chilies.

6. Build lettuce cups (or allow guests to) by piling noodles on top of the lettuce leaves. Top with mushrooms, sliced peppers, sesame seeds, and beet greens. Serve with dipping sauce.

Socca Bread
with Caramelized Onions

(Serves 4 as an appetizer)

This recipe is what you want on hand should you ever find yourself with company and no groceries (we've all been there!). All you need is chickpea flour and an onion and you'll have a delicious flat bread that can be used as an appetizer, a side dish, or a meal. No matter your guests' dietary needs or restrictions, this socca bread will deliver.

Ingredients

1 cup chickpea flour
1 tsp salt
1 tsp freshly ground black
  pepper
1 cup warm water
4 tbsp olive oil, divided, and
  more for brushing
1 sweet onion, sliced thinly

Directions

1. Put the chickpea flour in a bowl, and add salt and pepper. Add water, and whisk until there are no lumps. Add 2 tablespoons olive oil. Let the mixture sit for 15 minutes (or up to 12 hours covered on the counter). The batter should be creamy, not watery. If it seems too thin, then add more chickpea flour.

2. Preheat oven to 400°F.

3. While the oven heats, warm remaining 2 tablespoons of olive oil in an oven-safe frying pan (a cast-iron skillet is ideal), and add onions. Cook on medium-low for 20 minutes or until golden brown. Set aside half the onion to use as a topping. Arrange the remaining onions evenly over frying pan. Ensure the pan still has a good amount of oil to prevent the batter from sticking. Add more olive oil if necessary.

4. Pour the batter into the pan on top of the onions, tilting pan to ensure it covers the entire surface.

5. Bake for 10 to 15 minutes or until the socca is firm and the edges start to brown and pull away from the pan.

6. Set oven to broil. Brush the top of the bread with oil if it looks dry. Set the skillet a few inches away from the broiler and cook until golden brown. Stay close by—you don't want it to burn at this stage of the game!

7. Using an oven mitt, remove skillet from oven and use a spatula to loosen from the pan, then cut it into wedges and top with remaining onion. Serve hot right out of the pan (our preferred method) or transfer to a plate.

Buffalo Cauliflower-Pretzel Wings

(Serves 4 as an appetizer)

The crushed pretzels that coat these "wings" produce a crispy, salty layer that everyone goes nuts for. The fact that they're baked instead of fried means they're much healthier than traditional wings, plus no chickens had to lose a limb to make them! These are perfect Game Day appetizers and they don't last long, so make a bunch. We like to serve them with carrots, celery, and vegan ranch or blue cheese dressing.

Ingredients

1 cup chickpea flour
1 tsp salt
1 tsp garlic powder
1 tsp onion powder
1 cup non-diary milk
1 large head cauliflower, cut into bite-sized pieces
1 cup salted pretzels, crushed into very small pieces
1 cup buffalo wing sauce
Carrots and/or celery (optional)
Vegan ranch or blue cheese dressing (optional)

Directions

1. Preheat oven to 450°F.
2. In a large bowl, combine chickpea flour, salt, garlic powder, onion powder, and milk and whisk until combined.
3. Dip cauliflower in batter, then place each piece onto a parchment-lined baking sheet. The pieces can be close but not touching to ensure a perfectly crispy bite.
4. Bake for 20 minutes until they begin to brown slightly.
5. Meanwhile, place crushed pretzels into a bowl.
6. Remove the tray of cauliflower from oven and dip each piece into buffalo sauce to coat. Switch hands and dip in pretzel bowl and return to baking tray. Place back into oven for another 5 to 10 minutes until crispy. Remove from oven and serve with carrots, celery, and dip.

Chickpea Fries
with Roasted Sage Dip

(Serves 4)

Chickpea fries, or *panisses*, if you fancy yourself on vacay in the South of France, are surprisingly easy to make. This recipe calls for our chickpea "tofu," which is best if you allow to sit for a couple hours. Once fried, they are savory, crispy, and naturally packed with protein. Serve with a chilled glass or two of rosé.

Ingredients

1 batch Chickpea Tofu (page 155), sliced into thick french fry–sized slices
Oil, for cooking

For the Roasted Sage Dip

1 bunch fresh sage (about 1 cup), washed and dried
1 tbsp olive oil
½ cup vegan mayonnaise (store-bought or homemade, see page 158)
1 tsp sea salt
Fresh ground pepper, to taste

Directions

1. Preheat oven to 400°F.
2. In a deep skillet or pot, heat oil on medium-high heat.
3. Working in batches, lower fries into oil using a slotted spoon and fry for 3 to 5 minutes, turning occasionally, until golden brown. Remove from oil and place on a paper towel–lined plate. Allow to cool slightly.
4. Rub olive oil into sage leaves and place on a baking sheet. Cook for 6 to 8 minutes, turning halfway, until leaves are crispy and golden brown. Remove from oven, allow to cool, and crumble into small pieces.
5. In a small mixing bowl, add sage, mayo, and sea salt.
6. Serve fries with fresh ground pepper and sage dip.

Roasted Chickpeas (A Few Ways)
#1 Salty Sweet Roasted Chickpeas

Most people in Toronto will be familiar with Tiny Tom's Donuts, a Canadian National Exhibition staple. These mini deep-fried rings of goodness are saturated in icing sugar. Allow us to introduce you to the chickpea version! To cut sweetness, we have paired them with a salty sidekick because a salty-sweet combo is always a good idea. The key here is to divide the beans and dress them separately. Then reunite them in holy matrimony.

Ingredients

1½ cups cooked or canned chickpeas
2 tbsp olive oil
1 tsp coarse sea salt
2 tbsp icing sugar (or more if needed, you want to make sure the icing sugar does not absorb)
½ tsp cinnamon (optional)

Directions

1. Preheat oven to 450°F.
2. Rinse chickpeas then gently rub dry with a clean kitchen towel. Allow to air-dry until dry to the touch.
3. Coat with olive oil and cook for 25 minutes, shaking tray halfway through to rotate beans. After 25 minutes, turn off oven and leave the beans in the warm oven for another 10 minutes.
4. Divide chickpeas in half and place in two bowls. Add sea salt to one bowl and add icing sugar and cinnamon to the other bowl. Mix until evenly coated, then combine into one bowl of salty-sweet goodness!

#2 Sticky Fingers Spicy Tamarind Chickpeas

This tasty treat has a sour-ish bite to it that makes everyone come back for more. Despite the finger-licking nature of these peas, double-dipping into the bowl is a given. When it's baked, the tamarind creates an almost taffy-like coating that's irresistible.

Ingredients

1½ cups cooked or canned
   chickpeas
2 tbsp olive oil
¼ cup dried tamarind
1 cup boiling water
¼ cup brown sugar
1 tbsp chili flakes
1 tsp sea salt

Directions

1. Preheat oven to 450°F.
2. Pour boiling water over tamarind and let sit for 30 minutes.
3. Rinse chickpeas then gently rub dry with a clean kitchen towel. Allow to air-dry until dry to the touch.
4. Coat with olive oil and cook for 25 minutes, shaking tray halfway through to rotate beans. After 25 minutes, turn off oven and leave the beans in the warm oven for another 10 minutes. Remove and set aside.
5. Place water and softened tamarind into a high-speed blender and blend until smooth. Transfer to a small bowl and add sugar, chili flakes, and sea salt.
6. Stir tamarind sauce into chickpeas until well combined. Serve warm.

#3 Wasabi Chickpeas

Why should green peas get all the wasabi glory? It's time to give another legume a shot. Turns out chickpeas are up for the challenge.

Ingredients

1½ cups cooked or canned chickpeas
¼ cup tahini
1 tbsp soy sauce
2 tbsp wasabi paste

Directions

1. Preheat oven to 450°F.
2. Rinse chickpeas then gently rub dry with a clean kitchen towel. Allow to air-dry until dry to the touch.
3. Coat with olive oil and cook for 25 minutes, shaking tray halfway through to rotate beans. After 25 minutes, turn off oven and leave the beans in the warm oven for another 10 minutes.
4. In a medium bowl, whisk tahini, soy sauce, and wasabi paste. Coat chickpeas with mixture and stir until evenly covered. Then return to oven for 10 minutes or until crispy. Enjoy warm or cool.

CHAPTER 3
Food Trucks of the Future

Triple Threat Chickpea Poutine

(Serves 4)

We're not going to lie—this is definitely one of the more indulgent recipes in this book. So if you're watching your waistline, you may wish to partake in an extra session of calisthenics at some point today. Poutine is practically Canada's national dish, and a basic food group for any kid in college. Note: The "fries" use our chickpea tofu recipe and require a bit of preparation. If you're short on time and need to use fresh potatoes or frozen fries, don't fret. The cheese sauce and gravy also contain chickpeas so we've got you covered.

Ingredients

For the fries

2 batches of Chickpea Tofu (page 155), sliced into thick (approximately 1-inch) slices
Oil, for cooking

For the cheese sauce

¾ cup carrots, peeled and chopped
¾ cup sweet potato, peeled and chopped
¾ cup canned or cooked chickpeas
½ cup cashews, soaked for 10 minutes
3 tbsp nutritional yeast
1½ tsp sea salt
1 tbsp fresh lemon juice
¼ tsp smoked paprika
¼ tsp mustard powder
½ tsp garlic powder
½ tsp onion powder
⅓ cup olive oil
1 cup water

For the gravy

1 tbsp olive oil
1 small onion, diced
1 cup fresh mushrooms, sliced
2½ tbsp vegan butter or margarine
¼ cup chickpea flour
1½ cups vegetable broth
2 tbsp soy sauce
¼ tsp fresh ground black pepper
¼ cup packed fresh herbs such as parsley, cilantro, thyme (optional)

Continued on page 42

Directions

For the fries

1. In a deep skillet or pot, warm 1 inch of oil on medium-high heat.
2. Working in batches, lower fries into oil using a slotted spoon and fry for 3 to 5 minutes, turning occasionally, until golden brown. Remove from oil and place on a paper towel–lined plate. Allow to cool slightly.

For the cheese sauce

1. Bring a medium pot of water to boil. Add carrots and potatoes and allow to simmer for 10 minutes.
2. Combine all ingredients except oil and water in a high-speed blender. Begin to blend, slowly adding oil and then water, stopping to scrape down sides when necessary. Sauce should be thick and creamy, yet pourable.

For the gravy

1. In a small pot, warm olive oil on medium heat. Add onions and mushrooms and cook for 3 to 5 minutes. Remove from pot and set aside.
2. In the same pot on medium heat, whisk butter and flour for about 30 seconds. Add broth, soy sauce, and pepper. Continue to stir until you achieve desired thickness.
3. Return mushrooms and onions to the pot along with fresh herbs. Stir to heat through.

To Build the Poutine

1. Divide fries among four plates. Top with cheese sauce and hot gravy.

Italian Sandwich

(Serves 4)

Sometimes the mood calls for a giant, messy sandwich. This recipe is a vegan version of a classic fried chicken sandwich but with all the flavor and satisfaction of the real deal. It calls for tofu, eggplant, and Portobello mushroom, but it's not necessary to use all three. Try to find the biggest, freshest buns you can, and don't be shy with the marinara sauce. While it may not be first-date food, anyone who still loves you after watching you eat this sandwich is definitely a keeper.

Ingredients

3 tsp sea salt, divided
1 medium eggplant, sliced in ½-inch slices
1 cup chickpea flour
1 tsp garlic powder
1 tsp onion powder
1 tbsp Italian seasoning
½ cup almond milk
½ cup club soda
1 (350-g) block firm tofu, thinly sliced
2 large Portobello mushroom caps, thinly sliced
Vegetable oil for cooking
1½ cups marinara sauce, warmed
4 slices vegan cheese (we love Field Roast Chao brand)
4 large Kaiser buns

Directions

1. Sprinkle 2 teaspoons of sea salt onto eggplant slices (both sides) and let rest for 5 minutes. Rinse, drain, and pat dry with clean tea towel. Set aside.

2. Prepare batter by combining flour, garlic powder, onion powder, Italian seasoning, 1 teaspoon sea salt, almond milk, and club soda.

3. Heat 1 inch of vegetable oil on medium-high heat in a skillet.

4. Working in batches, dip eggplant, tofu, and mushrooms into batter and carefully place into oil. Using a slotted spoon, flip after 2 to 3 minutes and cook on other side. Pieces should be golden brown. Remove and place on a paper towel–lined plate.

5. Divide fried vegetables and tofu on base of Kaiser buns, along with cheese and warm marinara sauce. Top with other side of buns and let sit for a moment to allow cheese to melt.

Falafel Dog with Crispy Cabbage & Tahini Drizzle

(Makes 6 hot dogs)

When people think of chickpeas, falafels often come to mind. But who's to say they have to be balls tucked into a pita? This is a fun new way to enjoy falafel and a great opportunity to try different toppings.

Ingredients

½ head purple cabbage, thinly sliced
6 tbsp olive oil, divided
1½ cups cooked or canned chickpeas
1 red onion, chopped
1 bunch of parsley, roughly chopped (about ¾ cups firmly packed)
1 tbsp cumin
½ tsp chili powder
1 tbsp ground coriander
2 cloves of garlic, minced
1 tsp salt
1 cup all-purpose flour
4 hot dog buns

For the dressing

¼ cup tahini
Juice from ½ lemon
1 tbsp olive oil
1 tbsp soy sauce
1 clove garlic, minced
¼ tsp salt
1 tbsp chives or parsley, chopped
2 tbsp warm water

Directions

1. Preheat oven to 400°F.
2. Place cabbage on a lightly greased cooking tray and rub with 2 tablespoons olive oil. Roast for 30 minutes, stirring once or twice, until very crispy.
3. In a food processor, add chickpeas, onion, parsley, cumin, chili powder, ground coriander, garlic, salt, flour, and 4 tablespoons olive oil and pulse until combined.
4. Remove and form into hot dog–like shapes. Place on a parchment-lined baking sheet.
5. Bake for 20 to 25 minutes or until golden brown.
6. Meanwhile, make tahini dressing by combining all dressing ingredients in a glass jar with a lid and shake well. Set aside.
7. Place the dogs in buns, top with crispy cabbage, and drizzle with tahini dressing.

Fish-less Tacos
with Vegan Tartar Sauce

(Serves 4)

Fish tacos are so hot they're cool. But what if eating fish isn't your fancy? These fish-less tacos have you covered. They're quick to make, bursting with flavor, and will be the highlight of Taco Tuesday. When medium tofu is dipped in our perfect batter, coated with panko, and deep fried, it has a similar consistency to a flaky white fish.

Ingredients

1 batch Perfect Batter (see page 156)
1 cup vegan panko
2 (350-g) packages medium firm tofu (about 2 cups)
Vegetable oil, for frying
12 corn tortillas, warmed
Your favorite taco toppings such as salsa verde, shredded cabbage, chopped tomatoes, shredded lettuce, and vegan cheese

For the Tartar Sauce

3 tbsp vegan mayonnaise (store-bought or homemade, see page 158)
2 tsp sweet relish
1 tsp yellow mustard
½ tsp lemon juice

Directions

1. Place batter and panko in two separate bowls.

2. Meanwhile, drain the tofu. Cut into thirds (lengthwise) and wrap in a clean dry towel. Place under a heavy object like a book or a cutting board. Let sit for 10 minutes. Remove from towel and cut into small triangles or rectangles. Don't worry about perfect shapes. Get creative!

3. Heat oil on medium low in a skillet with a high edge (oil should be about 2 inches high). Dip individual pieces of tofu first into the batter and then lightly coat in panko. Place in hot oil for about 2 to 3 minutes, turning halfway, until crispy and golden. Place on a paper towel–lined plate. Repeat with all remaining pieces.

4. In a small bowl, combine mayonnaise, relish, mustard, and lemon juice.

5. Divide "fish" among warm corn tortillas. Top with toppings of your choice and drizzle with tartar sauce.

You'll-Never-Eat-Another-Burger Burger

(Makes 6 hefty burgers)

Whether or not you're vegan, once you try this burger, you may never go back. It's hearty, savory, and great for the planet. Initially, Heather's husband dared to develop a vegan burger without using chickpeas. But after months of hounding and calling his devotion into question, the chickpea version emerged.

Ingredients

1 cup white rice
2 tbsp olive oil
2 medium white onions, diced
2 large cloves garlic, minced
2 tsp sea salt
Juice from ½ lemon
1 tsp fresh ground pepper
½ cup cooked or canned
   chickpeas, mashed
¼ cup fresh basil, chopped
½ cup all-purpose or chickpea
   flour
½ cup quick oats
¾ cup firm tofu, crumbled
1 cup vegan panko or
   breadcrumbs
6 burger buns

Directions

1. Cook rice according to package instructions.
2. Preheat oven to 375°F.
3. In a large pot, heat olive oil on medium heat. Add onions, garlic, salt, lemon, and pepper and cook for 10 to 15 minutes until onions are translucent. Remove from heat and allow to cool.
4. Add rice, chickpeas, and fresh basil and combine well.
5. In a large bowl, combine flour, oats, and tofu. Add to rice and chickpea mixture and combine.
6. In a food processor, add half the mixture and process until smooth. Return to bowl and re-combine.
7. Shape into patties, dip into panko or breadcrumbs, and place on a parchment-lined baking sheet. Bake for 30 to 35 minutes, flipping halfway through.
8. Place on buns along with toppings such as lettuce, tomato, Dijon mustard, vegan mayonnaise, and pickles.

Soft Pretzels

(Makes 6 pretzels)

Close your eyes and imagine a world where soft pretzels are a healthy, protein-filled snack. Now open your eyes and look below! Soft pretzels are good to eat anytime, but try serving when guests come by so you can say, "Hold on a minute, let me get the soft pretzels from the oven." Serve with your favorite grainy mustard.

Ingredients

½ cup warm water, divided
1 tbsp maple syrup
½ tbsp active dry yeast
1½ cups all-purpose white
    flour, plus more for kneading
1 cup chickpea flour
1 tsp salt
2 tbsp oil
2 tbsp baking soda, for boiling
Coarse sea salt (topping)

Directions

1. Put ¼ cup warm water, maple syrup, and yeast into a small cup and stir until yeast dissolves. You want to see a fine foam on the surface (this can take a couple minutes). If yeast doesn't foam, you'll need to get fresh yeast.

2. In a mixing bowl, combine flour, salt, oil, yeast mixture, and an additional ¼ cup of water (for a total of ½ cup water). Mix and knead dough for about 5 minutes, adding white flour as needed.

3. Oil a large glass bowl and place ball of dough inside. Cover and let dough to rest for 40 minutes.

4. Preheat oven to 450°F. Prepare a cookie sheet with parchment paper. Set aside.

5. Uncover dough and knead it some more to reduce its size.

6. Boil water in a medium pot and dissolve 2 tablespoons of baking soda.

7. Meanwhile, cut the dough into 6 equal sections and roll each out to an approximately 15- to 18-inch long rope. Create a U-shape, then cross ends and press into dough to form a pretzel shape.

8. Drop pretzels, one at a time, into the pot of boiling water. Each should sink, then rise up. Boil about 1 minute and then lift out using a slotted spoon and place onto the cookie sheet. While still wet, sprinkle liberally with coarse sea salt. Take a sharp knife and cut a slit along sides of the pretzel.

9. Bake for about 8 to 10 minutes or until golden brown.

'Pea of the Sea Sandwich

(Serves 4)

Craving a tuna sandwich, but don't want to contribute to overfishing or worry about pesky mercury? This recipe is for you! Together with crumbled tempeh, crushed chickpeas have a texture similar to flaked tuna. And with a creamy dressing added, you'll never know the difference. High in protein, and full of flavor, this 'Pea of the Sea Sandwich will become a staple in your lunch rotation. Bonus: Kids love it, too!

Ingredients

1½ cups chickpeas, cooked or canned
⅓ cup crumbled tempeh
2–3 medium hearts of palm, chopped
¼ small red onion, diced
½ small red pepper, chopped
4 tbsp vegan mayonnaise (store-bought or homemade, see page 158) plus additional to spread on bread
1 tbsp Dijon mustard
1 tbsp fresh dill, chopped
Juice from ½ fresh lemon
Pinch of sea salt
4 green or red leaf lettuce leaves
4 fresh tomato slices (optional)
½ avocado, sliced thinly (optional)
8 slices whole grain bread or homemade Chickpea Bread (see page 161)

Directions

1. Place chickpeas in a large bowl and mash with the back of a fork or a potato masher. Texture should be chunky and you shouldn't see any whole chickpeas. Add crumbled tempeh, hearts of palm, red onion, and red pepper. Set aside.

2. In a small bowl, combine mayonnaise, Dijon, dill, lemon juice, and salt. Add to chickpea mixture and combine well.

3. Arrange on slices of bread with extra mayonnaise, lettuce, tomatoes, and avocado.

Sushi the Sequel: This Time It's Personal

(Serves 5–6)

We all love avocado and cucumber rolls, but sometimes we want to take things to the next level. Once you try the tomato "tuna" in this recipe, your hankering for sashimi will be gone for good. It's perfect for date night in or for entertaining discerning foodies. The sweet potato is dipped in our Perfect Batter, and then rolled in panko for a satisfying crunch. Be sure not to overcook the sweet potato—it should still be firm when it comes out of the oven, making it easier to slice. It will continue cooking once it's dipped in the batter and fried. Let's get rollin'!

Ingredients

1 large sweet potato, washed and wrapped in tin foil
1 cup Japanese white rice
¼ cup seasoned rice vinegar
1 batch Perfect Batter (see page 156)
4–5 Roma tomatoes
2 tbsp soy sauce
1 tbsp sesame oil
1 tsp fresh ginger, grated
½ tsp dried chili flakes or ½ tbsp sriracha sauce
Vegetable oil, for frying
5 sheets of nori
2 avocados, sliced
2½ tbsp vegan mayonnaise, store-bought or homemade (see page 158)
Additional soy sauce, sushi ginger, and wasabi for serving (optional)

Directions

1. Preheat oven to 400°F. Bake sweet potato for 20 minutes until it is firm but can be pierced by a fork. Allow to cool.

2. Cook rice according to package directions. Set aside and allow to cool slightly. Fold in rice vinegar.

3. Set a medium pot of water to a boil. Place tomatoes in rapidly boiling water for about 2 minutes. Remove with a slotted spoon and immediately place into a bowl of ice water. Peel skins off tomatoes and slice into long strips, scooping seeds out as you go and discarding.

4. Place tomatoes in a small bowl along with soy sauce, sesame oil, ginger, and chili flakes or sriracha. Using your hands, rub the sauce into the tomato until well marinated. Let sit for 10 minutes.

5. Peel sweet potato. Using a sharp knife, slice potato into ½-inch slices. Place batter and panko into two bowls.

6. Warm vegetable oil in a skillet on medium high-heat (oil should be about 1 inch deep in pan). Working in batches, dip the potato first into the batter, then into the panko, and drop gently into the oil. Cook for 3 to 4 minutes, turning midway, until potato is crispy and golden brown. Remove using a slotted spoon and place on a paper towel–lined plate.

7. Lay one sheet of nori on a sushi rolling mat, and spread with about ⅓ cup rice. Ensure there is a ½-inch space of visible nori remaining at the top.

8. In the center of the rice, lay about ½ tablespoon of mayonnaise, followed by a few slices of tomato "tuna," a few slices of avocado, and 2 long slices of fried sweet potato.

9. Carefully roll up sushi. When you get to the top, place a few dabs of water along the edge of the nori and seal the roll.

10. Remove roll from mat and place onto a cutting board. Using a sharp knife, cut into 8 even slices. Serve immediately with extra soy sauce, pickled ginger, and wasabi.

Pakoras

(Makes about 12 pakoras)

This appetizer, courtesy of Heather's food-savvy mother-in-law, is insanely tasty, and will blow you away with how easy it is to make. The best part about this dish is that you can use up whatever veggies are in your fridge, so it's a great way to reduce food waste. They fry up fast, so it's no trouble to throw them together when hungry guests show up unannounced (the nerve!). You may wish to double or triple the recipe if you're entertaining a crowd. A food processor works well for chopping up the veggies, but don't over process. Having some larger "chunks" gives the pakoras a nice visual appeal. And don't worry about the shapes being symmetrical—like snowflakes, every one will be different.

Ingredients

For the Pakoras

Vegetable oil, for frying
2 cups firm vegetables,
    chopped or thinly julienned
    (i.e., carrots, onions,
    cauliflower, broccoli,
    zucchini, beets)
2 shallots, thinly sliced
½ cup chickpea flour
1 tsp salt
½ tsp garam masala

For the sauce

¼ cup plain vegan yogurt
1 tbsp ketchup
1½ tsp mint sauce
½–1 tsp chile powder
Sea salt, to taste

Directions

1. Warm oil on medium-high heat in a deep pot (you can also use a home deep fryer if you have one). The oil should be about 2 inches high.

2. In a large mixing bowl, combine chopped veggies, shallots, chickpea flour, salt, and garam masala (clean hands work best to ensure the flour is fully coating the veggies). Form into 1½-inch round balls.

3. Using a slotted spoon, carefully lower the balls one at a time into the hot oil. You'll need to work in batches. Cook for 2 to 3 minutes, turning once or twice, until golden brown. Remove from oil and allow to cool by placing on a paper towel–lined plate.

4. In a small mixing bowl, make the sauce by combining yogurt, ketchup, mint sauce, chili powder, and salt.

5. Serve warm pakoras with dipping sauce.

Street Pad Thai

(Serves 4)

Who wouldn't want to be transported to the streets of Thailand where incredible food is available at every turn? If flying to Asia for dinner isn't in the budget, give this recipe a whirl. The sauce in this recipe is so good you might be tempted to drink it. But trust us, it will still be good once it's poured all over this better-than-takeout Street Pad Thai.

Ingredients

8 oz rice vermicelli noodles (half a package)
1 tbsp olive oil
1 cup broccoli, chopped
1 garlic clove, minced
¾ cup red pepper, diced
¼ cup tofu, cubed
¼ cup peanuts, chopped
1 lime, cut in wedges, for serving
2 green onions, diced, for serving
sprouted chickpeas, for serving (page 166)

For the sauce

¼ cup peanut butter or almond butter
½ cup chickpeas, cooked or canned
2 tbsp vegan mayonnaise, store bought or homemade (see page 158)
1 tbsp rice vinegar
4 tbsp soy sauce (or vegan fish sauce)
1 tsp minced ginger
1 tsp sugar
1 tsp salt
¼ cup avocado, or another neutral oil

Directions

1. Cook rice noodles according to package directions. Drain, rinse, and set aside.

2. Make the sauce by placing peanut butter, chickpeas, mayonnaise, rice vinegar, soy sauce or vegan fish sauce, ginger, sugar, salt, and oil in a high-speed blender. Blend until creamy and set aside.

3. Warm oil in a skillet over medium to high heat, add broccoli, garlic, and red pepper and cook for 5 to 7 minutes, or until tender.

4. Add drained noodles and tofu to skillet, and stir in sauce. Cook for 3 to 5 minutes, stirring until well combined and warmed through.

5. Divide among serving plates and garnish with peanuts, fresh lime, green onions, and sprouted chickpeas.

CHAPTER 4
Easy Like Tuesday Evening

Garbanzo Joes

(Serves 6)

You know those days when you want to eat something delicious, filling, good for you, quick to make, appealing to kids, *and* is easy on the planet? A tall order, but never fear, we have your back. These tangy, sweet, and Earth-friendly sandwiches are so simple to make, you likely have everything you need in your pantry already. So get messy and eat up! Note: This meal also works great in larger quantities, so feel free to double up the recipe. It's perfect for bringing to the cabin/cottage if you're the boss of a meal.

Ingredients

1 tbsp olive oil
1 medium onion, chopped
1 bell pepper in the color of your choice, diced
2 cloves garlic, minced
1 tsp cumin
1 tsp chili powder
½ tsp sea salt
1 cup tomato sauce
3 tbsp tomato paste
1½ cups cooked or canned chickpeas, mashed (use the back of a fork or a potato masher)
3 tbsp maple syrup (or sweetener of your choice)
1 tbsp yellow mustard
1 tbsp balsamic vinegar
1 tbsp nutritional yeast
1 tbsp hot sauce (optional)

Directions

1. Heat olive oil over medium heat and sauté onion for 4 to 5 minutes. Add pepper and garlic and cook for an additional 2 to 3 minutes. Add cumin, chili powder, salt, tomato sauce, tomato paste, and chickpeas.

2. Add maple syrup, mustard, balsamic, nutritional yeast, and hot sauce (if using). Let simmer for 3 to 4 minutes, allowing the flavors to get to know each other.

3. Slop evenly onto toasted buns and serve with something bubbly to drink.

Baked Mac & Cheese with Coconut Bacon

(Makes 4 servings)

This amped-up vegan version of traditional mac and cheese is delicious, creamy, and a real kid pleaser. Sneaky veggies and added protein from the chickpeas make caregivers feel virtuous (yay, you!). Bonus: It reheats well for the Spiderman thermoses the next day.

Ingredients

½ cup cashews, soaked for 10 minutes

4 cups macaroni

¾ cup carrots, peeled and chopped

¾ cup potato, peeled and chopped

¾ cup chickpeas

3 tbsp nutritional yeast

1½ tsp sea salt

1 tbsp lemon juice

¼ tsp smoked paprika

¼ tsp mustard powder

½ tsp garlic powder

½ tsp onion powder

⅔ cup olive oil

1 cup water

½ cup coconut bacon (you can find this in many health food stores or natural isles in your grocery store)

Directions

1. Cook macaroni according to package instructions.

2. Bring a medium pot of water to a boil. Add carrots and potatoes, reduce heat, and simmer for 10 minutes. Drain.

3. Add vegetables to a high-speed blender, along with chickpeas, soaked cashews, nutritional yeast, salt, lemon juice, paprika, mustard powder, and garlic and onion powders. Begin to blend, slowly adding oil and then water, stopping to scrape down sides when necessary. Sauce should be thick and creamy but pourable.

4. Add warm sauce to cooked pasta and combine well. Divide among bowls and add additional salt or fresh ground pepper. Sprinkle with coconut bacon.

Soba Noodles with Chickpeas & Ginger-Miso Dressing

(Serves 4)

Noodles would be our "one thing" if we found ourselves on a deserted island (with a genie who was granting food wishes). This recipe is healthy, eco-friendly, and delicious. It's a great option for weekday lunches, but fancy enough to impress dinner guests. The dressing can easily be made the day before to save even more time. Note: This recipe is also lovely with black chickpeas (shown in photo), if you happen to have some cooked and on hand. If you don't have a spiralizer, you can also use a sharp knife to thinly slice the veggies into matchsticks.

Ingredients

For the noodles

1 (8.8-oz) package (or similar size) buckwheat soba noodles
1 zucchini, spiralized
1 carrot, spiralized
1 cup chickpeas, cooked or canned
1 cup red cabbage, thinly sliced
1 yellow pepper, diced
2 tbsp toasted sesame seeds
Chili flakes, to taste (optional)

For the sauce

2 tbsp miso paste
2 tbsp vegan mayonnaise (store-bought or homemade, see page 158)
1 tsp agave
¼ cup soy sauce
1 garlic clove, minced
1 tbsp ginger, minced
2 tbsp tahini
2 tbsp apple cider vinegar
1 tsp sesame oil
¼ cup olive oil
⅓ cup water

Directions

1. Bring a medium pot of water to a boil. Add soba noodles and cook for 6 to 7 minutes. During last 2 minutes of cooking, add spiralized zucchini and carrots. Drain, rinse very thoroughly with fresh water, and set aside.

2. Make the sauce by combining all sauce ingredients except water in a high-speed blender. Blend until smooth, slowly adding water.

3. Place noodles, carrots, and zucchini in a large mixing bowl. Pour sauce on noodles and mix well.

4. Transfer to serving plates or bowls, and top with chickpeas, sliced cabbage, and yellow pepper. Sprinkle with sesame seeds and chili flakes (if using).

Lemon-Parsley Chickpea Penne

(Serves 4)

Chickpea pasta is turning up in health food stores across the nation. Not only is it gluten-free, but it's also packed with high-protein chickpeas, making it a healthier option for those with or without gluten sensitivities. If you can't find penne, feel free to choose another shape that suits your fancy. The intense lemon flavor in this simple pasta makes it pop and negates the need for an extensive ingredient list. This dish is best served when freshly cooked and still warm.

Ingredients

1 (227 g-package) chickpea penne
2 tbsp olive oil
3 cloves garlic, minced
½ cup parsley, chopped
1 tsp salt
1 tsp chili flakes
Zest from 1 lemon
1 can quartered artichoke hearts (about ½ cup)
1½ cup multicolored baby tomatoes, halved
Juice from 2 lemons
Fresh ground pepper, to taste
Vegan Parmesan or Chickpea Parmesan (see page 159), for serving (optional)

Directions

1. Cook pasta according to package directions. Drain, rinse, and set aside.

2. Meanwhile, warm olive oil on medium heat. Add garlic, parsley, salt, chili flakes, and lemon zest and sauté until garlic is golden brown.

3. Add artichoke hearts and tomatoes and cook until warmed through (tomatoes should be slightly softened). Add lemon juice.

4. Place pasta in a large serving bowl and toss with lemon mixture. Top with fresh ground pepper and vegan Parmesan. Serve immediately.

Lentil-Chickpea Dahl

(Serves 2)

There's a delightful simplicity to this dish. It's so easy to make and yet it's hearty, nourishing, and Earth friendly. Marrying chickpeas and lentils means your protein game is gonna be tight, so plan on running a marathon or solving all the world's problems after lunch. Serve on its own or with brown rice, quinoa, or warmed naan bread.

Ingredients

1 cup red or yellow lentils
3 cups water
2 cups spinach, packed
1 tsp salt
1 tbsp olive oil
1 clove garlic, minced
1 medium white onion, chopped
1 tbsp curry powder
1 medium red pepper, chopped
2 cups broccoli
½ cup chickpeas

Directions

1. Add lentils and water to a pot and bring to a boil. Reduce heat and simmer for 10 minutes (if using brown or green lentils, add an additional 5 minutes). Stir in spinach and salt and simmer for 5 more minutes. Set aside.

2. In a skillet, heat olive oil. Add garlic, onion, and curry powder and sauté for 3 minutes. Add red pepper, broccoli, and chickpeas and cook for 5 minutes.

3. Add mixture to pot of lentils and combine well.

Spaghetti Squash with Chickpeas

(Serves 2)

Spaghetti squash happens to be one of the most badass veggies around. It's seemingly low key from the outside, but once roasted and shredded, it's nothing short of a party in a gourd. With its mild flavor, all those long, tender noodles are perfect for adding a sauce of your liking. And if you're not too aggressive with the noodle removal, you can actually eat the finished product right out of the "shell." Bonus: No one is on dishes!

Ingredients

1 large spaghetti squash
1 tbsp olive oil
2 cloves garlic, minced
2 cups broccoli florets
1 red pepper, chopped
½ cup vegetable stock
1 cup chickpeas, canned or
    cooked
⅓ cup nutritional yeast
1 tsp sea salt
¼ tsp fresh ground pepper
Dried chili flakes (optional)

Directions

1. Preheat oven to 400°F.

2. Cut squash in half, lengthwise, and remove most of the seeds without disrupting the flesh of the squash. Place both sides, cut-side down, on a lightly oiled baking sheet and bake for 25 to 30 minutes, until squash can be easily pierced with a fork. Remove and allow to cool.

3. Heat olive oil in a skillet and add garlic, cooking for 2 to 3 minutes. Add broccoli and red pepper and continue cooking for an additional 3 to 5 minutes or until broccoli is bright green. Remove from heat and set aside.

4. Working separately with each half of the squash, gently run an upside-down fork over the squash, removing long strands or "noodles," and placing in a large bowl. Continue doing so until you've almost reached the bottom layer of the squash. Be careful not to pierce through; this layer makes for a handy bowl.

5. Add squash noodles to skillet along with vegetable stock and chickpeas. Stir or whisk in nutritional yeast and add salt and pepper. Bring to a boil, and let simmer for 5 minutes. Divide among hollowed-out squash "bowls" and garnish with additional salt, pepper, or dried chili flakes (if desired).

Tomato-Chickpea Salad with White Balsamic Vinaigrette

(Serves 4)

This is a stunning dish, especially in the summertime when tomatoes take over gardens by storm. We love to use a variety of tomatoes to shake things up. The salad can be thrown together in no time, so it's perfect for a weekday dish (even if you're only impressing yourself). Using a white balsamic vinegar keeps the focus on the brilliant colors of the fresh tomatoes and parsley. But if this is difficult to find, consider swapping for regular balsamic vinegar. To make this meal even speedier, you can substitute the chickpeas for the Marinated Chickpeas (page 158) if you have some ready to rock. Serve on a bed of crispy greens such as romaine, iceberg, or Boston.

Ingredients

4 tbsp olive oil, divided
1½ cups cooked or canned chickpeas
1 tbsp white balsamic vinegar
Juice from ¼ lemon
1 tsp ground cumin
1 green onion, finely diced
1 tsp sea salt
2 cups multicolored cherry (or small) tomatoes, halved or quartered
¼ cup fresh flat-leaf parsley, chopped
Fresh ground pepper, to taste

Directions

1. Warm 2 tablespoons olive oil over medium heat. Add chickpeas and cook for approximately 7 minutes, shaking pan to ensure they brown evenly on all sides. Remove from heat, transfer to a large bowl, and set aside to cool.

2. In a small dish, whisk together the remaining oil, balsamic vinegar, lemon juice, cumin, green onion, and salt.

3. Add tomatoes, parsley, and vinaigrette to the chickpeas and toss to combine. Add additional salt and pepper if desired and garnish with a few sprigs of fresh parsley. Serve on a bed of greens and top with fresh ground pepper.

Chickpea Pozole

(Serves 6)

Pulled jackfruit is the star of this authentic Mexican soup. It's spicy, savory, and perfect for a quick dinner or heated up as leftovers. Corn tostadas are ideal for scooping up the jackfruit, beans, and veggies. If you can't find hominy (made from dried corn) then just increase the amount of chickpeas in the dish. It's best served family style—with the toppings on the table—allowing everyone to help themselves.

Ingredients

2 (530-ml cans) jackfruit (yields about 3 cups)
1 (6.5-oz (186 ml) tin) chipotle peppers in adobo sauce (about ¼ cup)
1 tbsp olive oil
1 cup onion, diced
5 cloves garlic, minced
½ cup water
8 cups vegetable stock
1½ tsp salt
1 tsp oregano
1 medium zucchini, diced
2 cups cooked or canned chickpeas
1 cup canned hominy
Fresh cabbage, roughly chopped (for serving)
Radishes, sliced (for serving)
Sweet white onion, sliced (for serving)
Corn tostadas (for serving)

Directions

1. Drain jackfruit and place in a large bowl. Add chipotle peppers and adobo sauce. Using two forks or your hands, shred the jackfruit and rub the sauce from the peppers into the fruit.

2. Heat olive oil in skillet. Add onion and garlic and sauté for 5 minutes. Add jackfruit mixture and water. Allow to simmer for 10 minutes.

3. Meanwhile, bring stock to a boil. Add salt and oregano. Add zucchini, chickpeas, and hominy. Reduce heat to a simmer.

4. Add jackfruit mixture, and simmer for an additional 10 minutes. Ladle into serving bowls. Serve with your choice of toppings.

Chickpea Poke Bowl with Glass Noodles

(Serves 2)

Poke (pronounced "poh-kay") means to "slice" or "cut" in Hawaiian. Traditional poke is made with fish, but we've swapped this with sea-friendly tofu and veggies. It's simple to put together and can be as varied as you wish, so feel free to mix up ingredients to suit your fancy!

Ingredients

1 medium sweet potato
4 oz dried glass noodles
¾ cup purple carrots, sliced on diagonal
¾ cup smoked or firm tofu, cut into ½-inch cubes
⅓ cup pickled pepperoncini or pickled jalapeños
½ cup cooked or canned chickpeas
1 cup baby tomatoes, halved
1 shallot, thinly sliced
2 tbsp black sesame seeds

For Dressing

2 tbsp soy sauce
1 tbsp rice vinegar
1 tbsp maple syrup
Juice from ½ squeezed lemon
⅛ tsp ginger, minced
¼ tsp sesame oil

Directions

1. Preheat oven to 400°F. Wrap sweet potato in foil and bake for 30 minutes, until potato is tender but not mushy. Allow to cool completely. (Note: This step can be done in advance, up to 2 days before.)

2. Cook glass noodles according to package directions (typically 4 to 5 minutes in boiling water). Rinse, drain, and set aside.

3. Set a small pot of water to boil and add purple carrots. Allow to cook for 3 to 5 minutes until tender and bright in color. Note: You can also use as steamer for this step if you have one.

4. Meanwhile, make dressing by whisking together soy sauce, rice vinegar, maple syrup, lemon juice, ginger, and sesame oil. Set aside.

5. Divide glass noodles among bowls. Top with sweet potato, cooked carrot, tofu, pepperoncini or jalapeños, chickpeas, baby tomatoes, and shallot.

6. Top with dressing and sprinkle with sesame seeds.

Chick Nuggets

(Makes 12 nuggets)

Cutting down on meat consumption can mean missing out on eating certain blended and oddly shaped meat products. But never fear! These Chick Nuggets have a satisfying crunch outside and are deliciously flavorful inside. Plus, once you've covered them in ketchup, your little ones might just be converts.

Ingredients

½ cup panko or breadcrumbs
½ cup rolled oats
1½ cups cooked or canned chickpeas (reserve the aquafaba)
1 tsp salt
½ tsp garlic powder
1 tsp onion powder
2 tbsp nutritional yeast
¼ cup aquafaba

Directions

1. Heat oven to 375°F.
2. Place the panko or breadcrumbs on a rimmed baking sheet and bake until golden brown, about 5 minutes.
3. Place the oats in a food processor or blender and process to a fine flour.
4. Add the chickpeas to the food processor, along with salt, garlic, onion powder, and nutritional yeast. Pulse until crumbly. Add aquafaba and continue to mix until contents form a ball.
5. Divide the chickpea mixture into 12 equal portions and shape each one into a nugget. Coat each nugget completely in the toasted panko or breadcrumbs and place on a parchment-lined baking sheet.
6. Bake 15 to 20 minutes, or until crispy. Serve warm with your favorite dipping sauce.

Chapter 5
One Pot Wonders

Spanish Style Chickpeas & Spinach

(Serves 4)

This dish is super simple to make; however, you'll be surprised by how flavorful and complex the key ingredients become when married with the garlic and earthy spices. We love to serve this tapas-style on Jen's mom's homemade toasted sourdough bread, but it also tastes great on brown rice or quinoa (or just on its own). Serve for dinner and heat it up for a savory lunch the following day.

Ingredients

3 tbsp olive oil, divided
10 oz spinach (roughly 16 cups)
4 slices of bread, cubed
   (roughly 2 cups)
20 almonds, whole
3 cloves garlic, minced
1 tsp cumin
1 tsp smoked paprika
2 tbsp red wine vinegar
1½ cooked or canned
   chickpeas
½ cup marinara sauce
½ cup water
Salt and pepper, to taste

Directions

1. Heat 1 tablespoon olive oil on medium heat in a large skillet. Add half the spinach and sauté for about 2 minutes, or until wilted. Set aside and do the same with the remaining spinach, using an additional 1 tablespoon of olive oil. Remove from skillet and set aside.

2. In the same skillet, add cubed bread, remaining tablespoon of olive oil, and almonds. Cook until bread is golden brown and crispy. Add garlic, cumin, and smoked paprika and cook for 1 to 2 minutes.

3. Place bread and almond mixture into a food processor and add the red wine vinegar. Pulse until crumbly and return to skillet.

4. Add the chickpeas, marinara sauce, water, and wilted spinach. Cook for 2 to 3 minutes until heated through. Season with salt and pepper.

5. Serve on toast or grain of your choice.

Sunshine Soup

(Serves 6)

This wholesome and satisfying soup is perfect for a rainy or chilly day.
The smooth but hearty texture reminds us of a classic French-Canadian Pea Soup
but with a welcome sweetness owing to the roasted squash, apples, and cinnamon.
Serve with a green salad and a hunk of fresh bread.

Ingredients

½ large butternut squash,
    seeds removed
10 cups water
1 cup cooked or canned
    chickpeas
1 cup dried red lentils
3 apples, peeled, cored and
    chopped
2 tsp salt
½ tsp turmeric
¼ tsp cinnamon
⅛ tsp nutmeg
Freshly ground black pepper,
    to taste

Directions

1. Preheat oven to 400°F.
2. Place squash on a baking tray and bake for 60 minutes, or until soft when pierced with a fork. Remove, allow to cool, and scoop out inside flesh of squash. Set aside.
3. Meanwhile, place water, lentils, apples, chickpeas, salt, turmeric, cinnamon, and nutmeg in a pot and bring to a boil. Reduce heat and let simmer for 15 minutes. Add roasted squash and cook for an additional 5 minutes. Allow to cool and, working in batches, blend in a high-speed blender until smooth.
4. Return to pot, and, stir well to combine.
5. Divide among soup bowls, top with fresh ground pepper, and additional salt if desired.

Rockin' Moroccan Stew

(Serves 8)

This recipe is like a warm hug in a pot. Flavorful, earthy, and hearty.
It's a great dish to whip up on the weekend because of how well it reheats
for lunches and quick meals throughout a busy week. It can be enjoyed on
its own or served with short-grain brown rice or couscous.

Ingredients

2 tbsp olive oil
1 large onion, diced
4 cloves garlic, minced
1 tsp smoked paprika
1 tsp ground cumin
½ tsp ground coriander
½ tsp turmeric
½ tsp ground ginger
¼ tsp ground cinnamon
½ tsp ground black pepper
2 pinches cayenne pepper
1 (28-oz) can diced tomatoes
  (about 2 cups)
4 cups vegetable broth or
  water
1 tsp salt
1 large sweet potato, peeled
  and cubed
1½ cups chickpeas, cooked or
  canned
1 cup brown lentils
3 cups spinach
Juice from 1 lemon
Roasted slivered almonds (for
  serving)

Directions

1. In a large pot, heat olive oil. Sauté the onion until translucent. Add garlic and sauté for an additional minute. Add paprika, cumin, coriander, turmeric, ginger, cinnamon, black pepper, and cayenne pepper and stir until well combined.

2. Add the tomatoes, vegetable broth or water, and salt. Bring to a boil, and add sweet potatoes, chickpeas, and lentils. Cover and simmer for 30 to 35 minutes until the sweet potatoes and lentils are tender.

3. Turn off heat and stir in spinach until wilted. Stir in lemon juice. Sprinkle with roasted slivered almonds.

Chick 'N Noodle Soup

(Serves 4)

Chicken noodle soup has the reputation for curing all ills. Well, move over chicken, because this nourishing and comforting chick 'n noodle soup can make you feel like a million bucks! It's quick to make and a hit with grown-ups and kids alike. Freeze a batch for when a winter storm has you shut in or when you're feeling just a bit too lazy to cook.

Ingredients

2 tbsp olive oil
2 medium onions, chopped
4 cloves garlic, minced
4 medium carrots, thinly sliced
4 celery stalks, thinly sliced
6–8 sprigs fresh thyme
1 tbsp rosemary
2 bay leaves
1 tbsp sea salt
1 bunch Swiss chard, chopped
   (about 2 cups)
8 cups vegetable broth
6 oz capellini spezzati
1 cup cooked or canned
   chickpeas
Freshly ground black pepper,
   to taste
¼ cup parsley, chopped

Directions

1. Warm oil in a Dutch oven or large soup pot over medium heat until shimmering. Add the onions, garlic, carrots, celery, thyme, rosemary, bay leaves, and sea salt and sauté for 5 to 7 minutes or until softened but not browned.

2. Add Swiss chard, and cook for 2 minutes. Add the broth and bring to a boil.

3. Add the noodles and chickpeas and cook for about 8 minutes, or until the noodles are al dente. Taste and season with additional salt and fresh ground pepper as needed. Top with parsley and serve with crackers or bread.

Gnocchi with Chickpeas, Kale & Butternut Squash

(Serves 4)

Jen's brother-in-law starting making this for his wife, but he feels that it's too "intimate" to prepare for other acquaintances. We disagree, and insist that warm, creamy, bubbly, cozy, decadent foods can be shared with anyone . . . right? The sage, vegan butter, and Parmesan give this dish a wonderful richness. Serve alongside a fresh salad and warm bread and frequently hug the person sitting next to you as you're eating it.

Ingredients

2 tbsp vegan butter, divided
1 butternut squash, peeled
　　with the seeds removed and
　　cut into ½-inch pieces
3 cloves garlic, minced
3 tbsp fresh sage, chopped
½ tbsp chili flakes
½ tsp sea salt
1¾ cups vegetable broth
½ cup cooked or canned
　　chickpeas
1 bunch kale, chopped (about
　　8 cups)
Zest from ½ a lemon
1 (500-gram) package of
　　gnocchi
½ cup vegan Parmesan or
　　Chickpea Parmesan (see
　　page 159), divided
Juice from ½ lemon

Directions

1. In a large pot, melt 1 tablespoon vegan butter over medium heat. Add the squash and cook for about 8 minutes, stirring frequently, until golden and starting to soften. Add the garlic, sage, chili flakes, and salt, and cook for another 2 minutes.

2. Add the vegetable broth and, once simmering, reduce heat to low, add the chickpeas, kale, lemon zest, and gnocchi. Cover and let simmer for 5 minutes, stirring occasionally, until kale is wilted and gnocchi is tender.

3. Uncover and stir in 1 tablespoon of vegan butter, ¼ cup of Parmesan, and lemon juice.

4. Divided among serving bowls and top with remaining ¼ cup of Parmesan.

Simple Chana Masala

(Serves 4)

Finding the perfect Chana Masala recipe is no easy feat. Often, dishes like this are committed to memory only, and the thought of writing it down tarnishes the creative culinary act. Thankfully, Jen's neighbor is a Masala Master and was kind enough to let her in on his secrets. Turns out, the key to this dish is curry leaves (which can be found at a South Asian grocer) and a generous amount of coconut oil. Serve with basmati rice and warm naan bread.

Ingredients

½ cup coconut oil
1 medium onion, cut in long, thin slices
5 cloves garlic, minced
2½ tbsp ginger, minced
½ cup curry leaves, loosely packed (roughly 25 leaves)
1 tbsp turmeric
2 bay leaves
1 tsp mustard seeds
1 tbsp curry powder
2½ cups cooked or canned chickpeas
3 green Indian chilies whole, or to taste
½ tsp sea salt
2 medium tomatoes, diced
1 cup water
½ cup fresh coriander, for garnish

Directions

1. Warm coconut oil in a skillet on medium heat. Add onions, garlic, and ginger and cook on medium low heat for 5 to 6 minutes, until onions are soft. Stir in curry leaves, turmeric, bay leaves, mustard seeds, and curry powder.

2. Add chickpeas, chilies, salt, tomatoes, and water. Let simmer uncovered for 10 minutes until sauce is slightly reduced. Remove from heat.

3. Remove chilies and bay leaves, divide among bowls, and garnish with coriander.

Life-Affirming Ramen

(Serves 2)

Who doesn't love a warm bowl of noodles in a savory broth? This is the ultimate comfort food—delicious, soul soothing, and great for the planet. Together with miso paste, blended chickpeas help give this broth its cloudy hue. Chickpeas also amp up the soup's nutritional value by adding protein and fiber. Don't be shy with the chili flakes if you're looking to spice up your life a little.

Ingredients

4 cups vegetable broth
1 stalk lemongrass
1 tbsp ginger, grated
2 cloves garlic, minced
1 tsp sea salt
1 cup dried mushrooms
1 tbsp soy sauce
½ tsp sesame oil
½ tsp sriracha sauce
½ cup tofu, sliced thinly
4 oz ramen noodles
1 tsp olive oil
1 bunch bok choy, roughly
   chopped
2 tbsp pumpkin seeds
1 tbsp light miso paste
½ cup water
½ cup cooked or canned
   chickpeas
½ cup baby tomatoes, halved
1 ripe avocado, sliced
2 tbsp toasted sesame seeds
Crushed chilies (optional)

Directions

1. Preheat oven to 425°F.
2. Place broth in a medium pot and add lemongrass, ginger, garlic, salt, and mushrooms. Bring to a boil, reduce heat, and let simmer for 30 minutes.
3. Combine soy sauce, sesame oil, and sriracha in a small bowl. Place sliced tofu in marinade, covering completely, and let sit for 15 minutes.
4. Cook ramen according to package instructions. Drain and set aside.
5. Bake marinated tofu in oven for 10 minutes, flipping halfway. Set aside.
6. Heat olive oil in a skillet and add bok choy. Cook for 2 to 3 minutes until bright green.
7. Remove lemongrass from broth and discard. Remove mushrooms from broth, slice, and set aside. Place broth in a blender, along with miso paste, water, and chickpeas. Process until smooth.
8. Divide noodles evenly among two bowls and top with tofu, bok choy, sliced mushrooms, tomatoes, and avocado. Pour broth over dish, and sprinkle with pumpkin seeds, sesame seeds, and crushed chilies (if desired).

Italian Minestrone Soup with Neatballs

(Serves 6)

We like to make a big pot of this soup and enjoy it for several days. It's so wholesome and comforting that everyone wants more, so you may wish to double the recipe. Perfect for kids and grown-ups alike, it's lovely served alongside cut veggies and fresh bread. Black chickpeas are called for in this recipe, but regular ones will do just fine if that's all you have on hand.

Ingredients

For the Neatballs

2 tbsp ground flax
3 tbsp warm water
½ white onion, chopped
3 cloves garlic, minced
2 cups black chickpeas
1 tsp dried oregano
¼ cup fresh basil, chopped
¼ cup bread crumbs or vegan
    panko
2 tbsp vegan margarine
2 tbsp olive oil

For the Soup

1 (28-oz) can crushed tomatoes
4 cups vegetable stock
½ cup water
2 bay leaves
½ tbsp dried onion flakes
1½ tsp salt
3 carrots, peeled and sliced
¾ cup acini de pepe pasta

Directions

1. Place flax in warm water and allow to sit for 5 minutes, until thick and goopy.
2. Place onion, garlic, chickpeas, oregano, basil, bread crumbs or panko, and margarine in a food processor and process until well combined.
3. Using a teaspoon, shape mixture into tiny "Neatballs."
4. Heat olive oil in stock pot. Working in batches, cook balls for about 5 to 6 minutes, turning halfway, until golden brown and crispy. Remove from pot and set aside.
5. Using the same pot, place crushed tomatoes, vegetable stock, water, bay leaves, dried onion, salt, carrots, and pasta. Bring to a boil, reduce heat, and allow to simmer for 25 to 30 minutes.
6. Remove bay leaves. Place in serving bowls, topped with 8 to 10 Neatballs per bowl. Serve with fresh ground pepper and fresh bread if desired.

Pasta Fagioli
with Sneaky Chickpeas

(Serves 6)

This is an awesome wintertime warm-you-up soup. The blended chickpeas combined with the aquafaba help make a wonderfully thick and satisfying meal. Those who might not be as open to consuming whole chickpeas will be none the wiser to all the sneaky beans blended into this soup. Suckers.

Ingredients

½ cups cooked or canned
   chickpeas
½ cup aquafaba
1 tbsp olive oil
1 medium onion, chopped
3 garlic cloves, minced
2 celery stalks, chopped
2 carrots, chopped
3½ cups vegetable broth
1 (19-oz) can diced tomatoes
1 cup of your favorite marinara
   sauce
1 tsp dried oregano
2 bay leaves
½ tsp sea salt
1 cup small pasta noodles such
   as ditalini, orzo, or ancini di
   pepe
2 tbsp fresh basil, chopped
4 tbsp vegan Parmesan
   or Chickpea Parmesan
   (page 159)

Directions

1. Pour chickpeas and aquafaba into a blender and blend until smooth.

2. Warm oil in large pot over medium heat. Add onion, cooking for 4 to 5 minutes until softened. Add garlic and cook until fragrant. Add celery and carrots and cook for another 5 minutes.

3. Add vegetable broth, canned tomatoes, marinara, puréed chickpeas, oregano, bay leaves, and salt. Bring to a boil, cover, reduce heat, and let simmer for 15 minutes, stirring occasionally.

4. Remove bay leaves and use an immersion blender to purée the soup. Add pasta and continue to simmer for 10 minutes or until pasta is al dente.

5. Divide among serving bowls, and top with fresh basil and Parmesan.

CHAPTER 6
Showing Off

Earthy Vegetable Roast with BBQ Chickpeas & Tahini Dressing

(Serves 6–8 as a side dish)

Jen has many fond memories of getting together with friends and doing a giant vegetable grill-up, then they would gorge themselves (knowing that you can never really eat *too* many vegetables!). For this showstopper, we worked with our BBQ Master friends to create the perfect grilled dish. Top this masterpiece with the tahini dressing and, trust us, no one will be asking where the beef is.

Ingredients

For the veggies

1½ cups cooked or canned chickpeas
1 cup of your favorite barbecue sauce
3 medium zucchinis, sliced lengthwise into ½-inch slices
2 large eggplants, sliced into 1-inch slices
1 tsp sea salt
1 or 2 whole green cabbages, sliced into 6 large wedges each (ensuring base stays intact)
½ cup red wine vinegar
3 red, yellow, or orange bell peppers, quartered
2 large eggplants, sliced into 1-inch slices
2 large red onions, quartered
1 whole fresh lemon, juiced over grilled vegetables
Olive oil, for basting

For the Zucchini Marinade

2 tbsp olive oil
1 tsp dijon mustard
1 tsp maple syrup
1 lemon, juiced
1 tsp lemon zest

For the dressing

¼ cup tahini
½ lemon, juiced
1 tbsp olive oil
1 tbsp soy sauce or tamari
1 clove garlic, finely chopped
¼ tsp salt
1 tbsp chives or parsley, chopped
2 tbsp warm water

Continued on page 104

Ingredients

1. Combine chickpeas and the barbecue sauce and marinate the chickpeas for 1 hour or overnight, if possible.
2. Sprinkle zucchini and eggplant generously with salt and let sit for 3 to 4 minutes. Remove surface moisture with paper towel. Repeat on second side.
3. In a small bowl, whisk together zucchini marinade ingredients. Pour into large resealable bag or container. Place zucchinis into bag/container and allow to marinate for 20 minutes.
4. Meanwhile, make tahini dressing by combining all dressing ingredients in a glass jar with a lid and shake well. Set aside.
5. Preheat grill to high. Baste cabbage wedges with olive oil, and drizzle with red wine vinegar. Grill until edges begin to blacken and have grill marks. Put cabbage wedges on top rack to continue cooking while all other veggies are grilled.
6. Place marinated chickpeas in a large piece of tinfoil to create a bundle. Place on BBQ while grilling vegetables, allowing chickpeas to warm and caramelize. Stir occasionally.
7. Baste remaining veggies with olive oil (and/or leftover zucchini marinade) and grill for a few minutes. Each vegetable will cook at a slightly different rate, so look for grill marks and test for tenderness to know when each should be removed from the grill.
8. Plate all vegetables around the bundle of chickpeas, splash with lemon juice, and drizzle with tahini dressing.

Chickpea Pot Pies

(Makes 7 pies)

Who doesn't love their own personal pie? Your hands-off-my-food friends will love this recipe. Our savory chickpea pot pies have a wonderfully crispy crust and are jam-packed with a rainbow of delicious veggies and smothered in gravy. Throw down these pies for dinner and let the high fives roll in. Note: You'll need ramekins or something of a similar size.

Ingredients

2¼ cups all-purpose flour, divided
¾ tsp salt
1 cup vegetable shortening (at room temperature)
3 tbsp aquafaba
2 tbsp cold water
1 tbsp white vinegar
1 tbsp olive oil
1 small onion, diced
2 cloves garlic, minced
1 celery rib, diced
1 carrot, diced
1 white potato, diced into 1-cm cubes
½ red bell pepper, diced
1 tbsp nutritional yeast
2 tbsp soy sauce
½ tsp salt
¼ tsp pepper
1¼ cups vegetable broth
1 cup cooked or canned chickpeas
½ cup fresh or frozen green peas
1 tbsp sage, chopped
½ tbsp thyme leaves

Directions

1. Preheat oven to 400° F.
2. Combine 2 cups flour and salt. Using two knives, cut shortening into the mixture until crumbly and uniform. Add aquafaba, water, and vinegar into the mixture and stir until well combined and a dough-like consistency forms.
3. Divide dough into two balls, cover in plastic wrap, and chill in the fridge for 15 minutes.
4. Meanwhile, heat olive oil, add onion, and cook for 1 to 2 minutes until softened. Add garlic, celery, and carrot and sauté for an additional 2 to 3 minutes. Add potato and red pepper and cook, stirring frequently, for about 4 to 5 minutes until potato is tender but not mushy.
5. Add ¼ cup flour, nutritional yeast, soy sauce, salt, and pepper to the skillet and stir into the vegetables. Add vegetable broth and stir until combined, scraping all the browned bits from the bottom of the pan.
6. Add chickpeas, green peas, sage, and thyme and stir until combined. Remove skillet from heat.

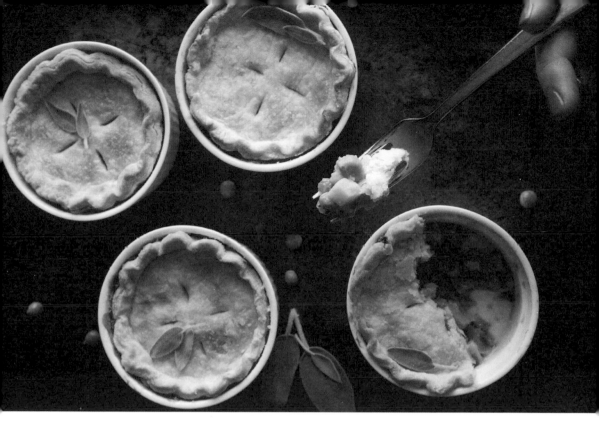

7. Remove dough from fridge and roll out on a lightly floured surface until uniform thickness, about ¼ inch thick.

8. Place ramekins upside down and cut around them with a butter knife, leaving ½ inch around all sides. Set dough aside and flip ramekins right-side up.

9. Divide the filling mixture between the ramekins and place a dough round over each, tucking in the sides. Pinch the edges or use a fork to create a pattern around the sides. Cut a slit in the middle to allow steam to escape.

10. Place ramekins on a baking sheet and bake for about 30 minutes, until crust is golden and filling is bubbling. Let sit for 5 minutes before serving.

Gorgeous Green Salad with Sprouted Chickpeas & Caesar Dressing

(Serves 4–6 as a side dish)

Sometimes it's nice to treat your guests (and yourself) to a fresh, heart-healthy meal that doesn't make them feel like they've overdone it. This salad lets your people know that you care about more than their great taste in music and sense of humor. This salad is bursting with flavor and full of earth-friendly ingredients. Try to hit up your local farmers' market for the freshest greens you can find. Your taste buds (and friend buds) will thank you.

Ingredients

For the salad

1½ cups brussels sprouts, cut in half
1 tbsp olive oil
¼ tsp coarse sea salt
1 bunch red leaf lettuce, washed and broken into bite-sized pieces
2 cups fresh arugula
1 cup Swiss chard, washed and torn into bite-sized pieces
¼ cup fresh basil, chopped
¼ cup fresh cilantro, chopped
½ cup fresh green peas
2 large ripe avocados, pitted and sliced
½ cup shelled pistachios
⅓ cup sprouted chickpeas (page 166)

For the dressing

½ cup cashews, soaked for at least 20 minutes
⅓ cup canned or cooked chickpeas
Juice from 1 lemon
3 caper berries (or 6 capers)
3 large cloves garlic, minced
1 tbsp nutritional yeast
¼ tsp sea salt
½ tbsp soy sauce
⅛ tsp fresh ground pepper
¼ cup olive oil
¼ cup water

Directions

1. Preheat oven to 400°F. Place Brussels sprouts on a baking sheet and drizzle with olive oil. Using your hands, massage the oil into the sprouts. Sprinkle with sea salt. Bake for 15 minutes, turning once or twice, until golden brown and crispy.

2. In a large serving bowl, mix lettuce, arugula, Swiss chard, basil, and cilantro. Top with fresh green peas, avocado slices, pistachios, sprouted chickpeas, and Brussels sprouts.

3. Make dressing by adding lemon juice, caper berries, garlic, nutritional yeast, salt, soy sauce, and pepper to a blender. Begin blending and slowly add oil and then water. Continue to blend until smooth and creamy.

4. Pour on top of salad, toss, and serve.

Quinoa with Chickpeas & Cilantro-Pepita Pesto

(Serves 4)

This dish is bursting with flavor and couldn't be simpler. It's a high-protein meal that packs a nutritional punch with both quinoa and chickpeas. The cilantro pesto will have you feeling tempted to eat it straight out of the food processor (please don't, safety first!). Enjoy this as a main course along with a salad, or pack for lunches during the workweek. It's great served warm or cold.

Ingredients

½ cup pepitas (raw pumpkin seeds)
1½ cups water
1 cup quinoa, rinsed and drained
2 cloves garlic, peeled, halved
1 tsp ground cumin
1 cup cilantro leaves, washed, dried
½ small jalapeño, seeded, halved
3 tbsp olive oil
1 tsp sea salt
1 tsp fresh lime juice
½ cup Pickled Chickpeas (page 163) or cooked/canned chickpeas
1 red bell pepper, diced
2 green onions, thinly sliced

Directions

1. Preheat oven to 450°F. Place pepitas on a baking sheet and toast for 5 to 7 minutes, occasionally shaking pan.

2. In medium pot, bring water to boil over high heat. Add quinoa, reduce heat, and simmer for 15 minutes until water is absorbed. Remove from heat, cover, and let sit for 5 minutes.

3. Add pepitas to a high-speed blender or food processor, along with garlic, cumin, cilantro, jalapeño, olive oil, salt, and lime juice. Process until smooth.

4. Fluff quinoa with a fork, transfer to a large serving bowl, and mix in cilantro pesto, pickled chickpeas, and red peppers. Top with green onions.

Teriyaki Chickpea Tofu

(Serves 2)

If you're in the mood for Japanese food, but find the thought of rolling sushi to be daunting, this Teriyaki Chickpea Tofu dish is for you! You'll be surprised by how quickly you can re-create such complex flavors in your own kitchen. The recipe below uses our chickpea "tofu," which can be made in advance so it's ready to go. If you don't have any on hand, feel free to substitute for regular firm tofu and just add a ½ cup of cooked or canned chickpeas.

Ingredients

1 cup Japanese white rice
2 tbsp vegetable oil, divided
2 cups Chickpea "Tofu" (page 155) or firm tofu, cut into bite-sized cubes
¼ cup chickpea flour
3 tbsp soy sauce
2 tbsp seasoned rice vinegar
2 tbsp sake
2 tbsp granulated sugar
1 tsp chili flakes
½ tsp cornstarch
½ tbsp fresh ginger, minced
1 large carrot, sliced into diagonal coins
1 red bell pepper, diced
½ crown broccoli, chopped
½ cup chickpeas, cooked or canned (optional)
2 tbsp cashews

Directions

1. Cook rice according to package instructions.

2. Warm 1 tablespoon of oil in skillet on medium heat. Coat tofu cubes in flour. Place in oil and cook for 2 to 3 minutes, turning frequently, until crispy and golden brown. Remove from pan and set aside.

3. In a small bowl, whisk together soy sauce, rice vinegar, sake, sugar, chili flakes, and cornstarch.

4. Heat remaining oil in pan and add ginger, cooking for about a minute. Add carrots, pepper, broccoli, chickpeas, and cashews, and cook for an additional 3 to 4 minutes. Add soy sauce mixture and cook for 1 to 2 minutes.

5. Add rice to serving bowls and top with vegetables, followed by crispy tofu.

Spaghetti & Meat-less Balls

(Serves 4)

This take on traditional meatballs is perfect for entertaining discerning foodie friends. The flavor and texture of the meat-less balls are enhanced by fresh herbs and spices, and while browning them at the end of baking isn't absolutely necessary, this step provides an irresistible crispiness. Serve with a green salad and fresh bread.

Ingredients

For the Meat-less balls

2 tbsp ground flax
5 tbsp warm water
2 tbsp olive oil
½ medium sweet white onion, minced
2 cloves garlic, minced
1½ cups chickpeas, cooked or canned
1 cup Italian breadcrumbs, divided
½ cup parsley, chopped
½ cup basil, chopped
1 tsp salt

For the Spaghetti

8 oz spaghetti or linguine noodles
2 cups marinara sauce
4 tbsp vegan Parmesan or Chickpea Parmesean (page 159)
Fresh ground pepper, to taste

Directions

1. Combine ground flax and water in a small bowl and let sit for 10 minutes.
2. Preheat oven to 350°F.
3. Cook spaghetti or linguine according to package instructions.
4. In a skillet, heat 1 tablespoon olive oil on medium heat. Add onion and cook for 3 to 5 minutes until fragrant, then add garlic and cook for 1 more minute. Remove from heat and set aside.
5. In a food processor, combine chickpeas, ½ cup of the breadcrumbs, sautéed garlic and onion, parsley, basil, flax mixture, and salt. Process until well combined.
6. Scoop out one heaping tablespoon at a time and roll into balls. Place about 1 inch apart on an oiled baking sheet. Bake for 15 to 20 minutes until browned and slightly crispy. Remove from oven.
7. Heat remaining tablespoon of olive oil on medium heat in the same skillet you used for the garlic and onions. Cook chickpea balls for 3 to 5 minutes, turning often until they are crispy and golden brown.
8. Warm marinara sauce in a medium pot.
9. Divide cooked noodles among serving plates, top with marinara sauce, meat-less balls, Parmesan, and fresh ground pepper. Serve with salad and bread.

Rollercoaster Pasta
with Savory Mushroom Sauce

(Serves 6)

This dish brings us back to our Chef Boyardee days when happiness was measured by the number of meatballs you scored from the can of "Roller Coasters" at lunch. Now that we're full grown, we tend to get more excited by fancy mushrooms than by mini processed meatballs. This dish is rich, savory, and a gorgeous choice for a dinner party. If you have access to a cast-iron pan, use that—it's great for scraping up the sweet, crispy bits after caramelizing the onions.

Ingredients

½ cup dried mushrooms (e.g., shiitake, porcini, chanterelle)
1 cup water, boiling
1 (16-oz) package chickpea reginette (we used Maria's Healthy Noodles for this recipe)
2 tbsp olive oil, divided
1 medium red onion, sliced thinly
1 cup crimini mushrooms, sliced
¼ cup red wine
¼ cup chickpea flour
2 cups vegetable broth
1 bay leaf
2 tbsp soy sauce
1 tsp salt
¼ cup vegan Parmesan or Chickpea Parmesan (page 159) or hard vegan cheese, shaved

Directions

1. Place dried mushrooms in a bowl and cover with 1 cup boiling water. Let soak for 10 minutes, remove from water (don't discard water), and slice.

2. Cook pasta according to package instructions.

3. On medium high, heat 1 tablespoon olive oil in a skillet. Add onion and cook on low for 15 to 20 minutes until slightly caramelized, scraping up bits on the bottom of the pan. Remove onions from skillet and set aside.

4. In the same skillet, heat remaining 1 tablespoon of olive oil. Add soaked mushrooms and crimini mushrooms and cook for 3 to 4 minutes until golden brown. Add red wine and let simmer for 5 minutes.

5. Return onions to skillet. Add flour and coat mushrooms and onions, cooking for 2 to 3 minutes. Slowly pour in broth and reserve water from soaked mushrooms, using a whisk to break up chunks of flour. Add bay leaf, soy sauce, and salt and let simmer for about 15 minutes, until liquid thickens.

6. Add sauce to cooked pasta and top with Parmesan or hard cheese. Serve immediately.

Risotto with Mushroom, Spinach & Crunchy Chickpea Topping

(Serves 4)

Risotto is always a crowd pleaser. Plus, you can really look like you're working hard on the meal when your guests watch you stir and stir . . . and drink wine . . . and stir. The crunchy protein-packed topping with a hint of spice is the perfect addition. Serve with warm bread, a green salad, and whatever wine you didn't polish off while cooking.

Ingredients

For the Topping

½ cup cooked or canned chickpeas
2 tbsp olive oil
¼ tsp salt
1 tsp smoked paprika
Cayenne (to taste)

For the Risotto

3½ cups vegetable broth
2 tbsp extra-virgin olive oil
½ sweet onion, chopped
2 cloves garlic, minced
4 cups shiitake mushrooms sliced
   (or mushroom of your choosing)
1 tsp salt
1½ cups arborio rice
1 cup dry white wine
1 tbsp miso paste
2 tbsp nutritional yeast
3 packed cups baby spinach leaves

Directions

For the Topping

1. Preheat oven to 450°F.
2. Rinse chickpeas then gently rub dry with a clean kitchen towel. Allow to air dry until dry to the touch. The drier they are, the crispier they will get! Lightly mash the chickpeas with a fork or potato masher. Don't worry about removing the skins; this will make them crunchier.
3. Drizzle with olive oil, then add salt, smoked paprika, and cayenne. Use your hands to mix everything through, then lay flat for roasting.
4. Roast for 25 minutes, shaking tray halfway through to rotate beans. After 25 minutes, turn off oven and leave the beans in the warm oven for another 10 minutes.
5. Place in bowl and set aside.

For the Risotto

1. Add vegetable stock to a pot and begin to warm on medium heat.

2. In a skillet, set oil over medium heat and sauté the onion for 3 to 5 minutes, or until soft. Add garlic and cook for another minute, then add mushrooms until they begin to shrink down. Add salt.

3. Add the rice and cook for 2 to 3 minutes, until it's glossy and coated with oil.

4. Start to add wine, ½ cup at a time. Stir frequently until all wine is absorbed.

5. Start to add broth, ½ cup at a time. Stir frequently until all broth is absorbed (the more you stir, the creamier it will become). The mixture should be neither soupy nor dry. Add more broth if necessary.

6. After 20 minutes, taste the rice to ensure it is cooked. Once the rice is at the desired tenderness, stir in the miso (you might need to add some water to the miso to make it easier to mix in) and nutritional yeast, then add the spinach and stir until wilted.

7. Remove from heat and serve with a generous helping of the Crunchy Chickpea Topping.

Acorn Squash Salad with Black Chickpeas, Roasted Grapes & Lemon-Tahini Dressing

(Serves 4–6 as a side dish)

This salad is a tabletop showstopper. You may actually hear your friends whisper "masterpiece" as you give off an air of *oh, this old thing*? It's surprisingly easy to pull together, but don't try to skimp on steps. Massaging the kale may sound creepy, but just do it—the difference is dramatic. This dish is best served in the largest bowl or platter you own, so all the good stuff is visible.

Ingredients

For the Salad

1 small bunch red grapes (approximately 2 cups)
1 medium acorn squash, cut into ½-inch slices
1 tbsp olive oil
3 tbsp pine nuts
¾ cup black chickpeas (or regular chickpeas), cooked or canned
1 bunch red kale, stems removed (approximately 4 cups)
1 bunch green kale, stems removed (approximately 4 cups)
Pinch of salt and pepper
¼ cup vegan Parmesan or Chickpea Parmesan (see page 159)

For the dressing

¼ cup olive oil
Juice from 1 large lemon (about ¼ cup)
2 tbsp tahini
1 large clove garlic, minced
½ tsp fine sea salt
Freshly ground black pepper (to taste)
½ cup parsley
½ cup cilantro

Directions

1. Preheat oven to 350°F.
2. Place bunches of grapes on a baking tray. Place squash rings on another tray and brush both sides with olive oil. Sprinkle with salt and pepper. Bake grapes for 20

minutes until they begin to expand and their juices begin to run. Bake squash for 30 minutes until soft.

3. Once grapes and squash are cooked, place pine nuts on a tray and toast for 5 minutes, shaking pan every few minutes to prevent burning.

4. In a high-speed blender, add all dressing ingredients and pulse until well combined. Set aside.

5. Place red and green kale leaves in a large bowl. Using an action similar to kneading dough, massage the kale for about 3 to 4 minutes, or until the leaves are softened.

6. Pour dressing on kale and top with roasted squash rings, grapes, toasted pine nuts, and Parmesan. Season with additional salt and pepper to taste.

Chickpea Mushroom Loaf

(Serves 4)

Both Heather and her husband have fond memories of meat loaf with red sauce when they were kids (soul mates!). So this vegan take on the classic meatloaf obviously includes the red topping like the good old days. The fresh herbs and garlic make this dish burst with flavor. It's perfect for a main course, served with steamed veggies or salad. But it's also great the next day, sliced and served cold on sandwiches.

Ingredients

For the loaf

2 tbsp olive oil, divided
½ cup onion, diced
1 clove garlic, minced
1 cup carrots, peeled and roughly chopped
¾ cup cashews, soaked for 10 minutes
½ cup breadcrumbs
1½ cups cooked or canned chickpeas
1 tbsp fresh basil, chopped
1 tbsp fresh parsley, chopped
1 tsp fresh sage, chopped
1 tsp nutritional yeast
1½ tsp sea salt

For the topping

2 tbsp brown sugar
4 tbsp ketchup
1 tsp dry mustard

Directions

1. Preheat the oven to 350°F.

2. In a saucepan, warm 1 tablespoon of olive oil on medium heat. Cook onion and garlic for 2 to 3 minutes until soft.

3. Bring a medium pot of water to boil and add carrots. Let simmer for 8 to 10 minutes until very soft. Drain, rinse with cold water, and mash with potato masher or back of fork. Set aside.

4. Grind the cashews in a food processor and mix with the breadcrumbs in a large bowl.

5. Blend chickpeas in a food processor or high-speed blender until crumbly. Add to bowl, along with carrots and fresh herbs. Add nutritional yeast, salt, onion, and garlic into the mixture.

6. Heat the remaining tablespoon of oil in a skillet and sauté the mushrooms until soft.

7. Grease a 9 x 5-inch loaf pan, then press in half the chickpea mixture. Cover with a layer of mushrooms and top with the rest of the chickpea mixture, pressing down as well. Cover and bake for 60 minutes.

8. Remove from oven, let sit for 10 minutes to cool. Flip pan upside down onto a cutting board.

9. In a small bowl, combine ingredients for topping. Warm in a small sauce pan, and evenly spread on loaf. Slice, serve, and enjoy!

Hearty Farmer's Pie

(6–8 servings)

This dish is a grand slam in terms of nutrition, taste, and the effort required to make it. It'll quickly become part of your weekly rotation, as it's perfect for satisfying a hungry crowd. The whiskey is a lovely addition, bringing out a rich, smoky flavor in the dish. This recipe makes a good amount for a dinner party, but also reheats well if you're preparing for a smaller crowd (or a hungry you).

Ingredients

3 large sweet potatoes, peeled and cut into ½-inch chunks
1 cup lentils
2 tbsp vegetable oil
1 medium onion, chopped
1 clove garlic, minced
2 cups fresh or frozen mixed vegetables (e.g., broccoli, carrots, corn, peas, mushrooms)
1½ cups cooked or canned chickpeas, mashed
3 tbsp chickpea flour
⅓ cup whiskey (optional, but tasty) or water
1 vegetable bouillon cube
3 tbsp soy sauce
8 sprigs fresh thyme, leaves removed
Salt and pepper, to taste
2 tbsp vegan margarine
⅓ cup soy or almond milk

Directions

1. Preheat oven to 350°F.

2. Set both a large pot and medium pot of water to boil. In large pot, add sweet potatoes and let simmer for 20 minutes, or until tender. Drain and set aside. In small pot, add lentils and cook for 6 to 8 minutes, or until tender. Drain and set aside.

3. Meanwhile, in a large skillet, warm oil over medium heat. Cook onion and garlic for 1 minute or until onions are soft. Add the veggies and cook for 5 minutes (if using frozen veggies, increasing cooking time by a few minutes). Add the lentils and chickpeas and cook for an additional 2 to 3 minutes. Sprinkle flour over the mixture and mix well. Add whiskey or water, bouillon cube, soy sauce, thyme, and season well with salt and pepper. Cook, stirring, for 2 to 3 minutes. Set aside.

4. In a medium bowl, mash sweet potatoes with margarine and soy or almond milk.

5. Spoon chickpea/lentil mixture into a 9 x 13-inch pan. Top with sweet potato. Cover and bake for 30 minutes or until bubbly. Let stand for 5 minutes before serving.

CHAPTER 7
Sweet As . . .

Lemon Meringue Pie

(Serves 6)

Heather's Nana did a million things right (including traveling the globe extensively, well into her senior years). Making a mean lemon meringue pie topped the list. It was the most requested treat for birthdays and celebratory occasions and it's no wonder why. It was bursting with lemony goodness, and the meringue had such massive peaks they demanded their own time zone. The vegan version of this dish would make her proud. You'd never know it's missing milk or eggs (we promise). Note: Agar-agar is a plant-based alternative to gelatin and helps keep the lemon filling nice and sturdy.

Ingredients

¾ cup aquafaba
½ cup granulated sugar, plus 1¼ cups
½ cup corn flour
¼ tsp agar-agar
¼ tsp sea salt
¼ cup soy milk
1 cup water
¾ cup fresh lemon juice
1½ tbsp lemon zest
1 (9-inch) vegan pie crust

Directions

1. Preheat oven to 350°F.
2. Pour aquafaba into a large mixing bowl. Using electric beaters or a stand mixer, mix liquid for 10 to 15 minutes until stiff peaks form. Throughout this process, slowly add ½ cup sugar, 1 tablespoon at a time. When it's set, you should be able to tip the bowl upside down without the contents falling out. Set aside.
3. Add 1¼ cups sugar, corn flour, agar-agar, sea salt, soy milk, water, lemon juice, and lemon zest to a sauce pan. Bring to a boil, stirring constantly, until mixture is very thick.
4. Pour mixture into pie crust, spread evenly, and allow to cool for 20 minutes.
5. Place meringue topping evenly on pie, creating peaks and swirls with the back of a spoon (don't have too much fun, this is serious business).
6. Carefully place in oven and bake for 30 minutes until peaks are golden brown. Allow to cool slightly, and serve.

Crème Brûlée

(makes 4 pots)

Crème Brûlée is the one thing people feel an almost moral obligation to order off a menu. Think about it—if a chef has gone through the trouble of scraping out the inside of a vanilla bean, what kind of a person would you be by *not* ordering it? Traditional crème brûlée is full of dairy and eggs, but our vegan version will blow your mind with its similarities—rich, decadent, creamy on the inside, with a perfect crispy coating on top (lean in close when you break the topping with your spoon to hear that feel-good sound). It may take you some time to get used to torching your food, but you'll also feel a bit badass as you're doing it—sort of like a fire-breathing dragon, but in the kitchen. Note: You'll need small dishes or ramekins and a kitchen torch for this recipe.

Ingredients

1 vanilla bean, sliced lengthwise with seeds from inside scraped out (keep the seeds, discard the shell)
½ cup cooked or canned chickpeas
⅛ tsp agar-agar
1 (350-gram) package organic soft tofu (about 1 cup), strained and squeezed of excess water (cheesecloth works well for this)
¾ cup organic sugar, divided
½ tsp sea salt
1½ tbsp nutritional yeast
2 tsp cornstarch
1 cup full-fat coconut milk

Directions

1. In a high-speed blender or food processor, add all ingredients except ½ cup sugar. Blend until creamy.

2. Pour blended mixture into saucepan and cook over medium heat until thick, stirring constantly, for about 5 minutes.

3. Divide evenly among ramekins and allow to cool. Cover and place in fridge for at least 5 hours but preferably overnight.

4. Before serving, divide remaining sugar among dishes and torch until bubbly and golden brown.

Frozen Strawberry Cake

(Serves 8)

Some interesting culinary trends emerged in the 1970s. Like the Easy Bake Oven, for example. This first foray into baking was often coupled with an ever-present danger—and an inevitable sadness when the mini mixes ran out, forever. The strawberry frozen cake however, was a seventies high-five. As a shower gift, Heather's mom was given the "new" *Better Homes Cookbook*, starring the recipe that inspired our dish. Your guests will love it and it'll bring you back to when you wore corduroy overalls and rocked a bowl cut (thanks, Mom!?).

Ingredients

1 cup flour
¼ cup brown sugar
½ cup chopped walnuts
½ cup vegan margarine, melted
1 cup aquafaba
⅔ cup granulated sugar
2 cups fresh strawberries, sliced
2 tbsp lemon juice

Directions

1. Preheat oven to 350°F.
2. In a mixing bowl, combine flour, brown sugar, chopped walnuts, and margarine (hands are good tools for this task). Spread crumb mixture onto a baking sheet and bake for 20 minutes, stirring occasionally. Remove from oven and allow to cool slightly.
3. Sprinkle ⅔ of the crumbs in 9 x 13-inch baking dish to form a loose crust.
4. In a large mixing bowl, combine aquafaba and granulated sugar and, using beaters or a stand mixer, whip for 10 to 15 minutes. Once stiff peaks form (you should be able to tip the bowl upside down with contents staying put), set aside.
5. In a food processor, pulse berries and lemon juice until coarse. Combine berry mixture with aquafaba mixture. Pour into an ungreased baking dish (aquafaba doesn't like oil) and sprinkle with remaining crumbs.
6. Freeze at least 6 hours. Top with fresh strawberries, blueberries, or raspberries.

No-Bake Power Balls

(Makes approximately 15 balls)

Going to visit friends who just had a baby? Bring some Power Balls. Heading out for the day and don't want to have your blood-sugar levels crash? Power Balls. Don't want to be around a cranky, hungry child? Power Balls! Bottom line, these are great to have on hand so you don't end up eating anything and everything in sight. Make a double batch and freeze half. Present you will thank past you.

Ingredients

1 cup dates, pitted (if dry, soak in warm water for 5 minutes, drain well)
½ cup chickpeas, cooked or canned
1 cup rolled oats
1 tbsp chia seeds (or flax or hemp seeds)
3 tbsp peanut or almond butter
¼ cup dark chocolate, roughly chopped

Directions

1. Blend dates in a food processor until smooth and they form a ball.
2. Add chickpeas, oats, chia seeds, and peanut butter or almond butter, and pulse until well combined but still chunky. You may need to stop and scrape down the sides to ensure it properly blends. Add chocolate at the end and blend for a short time (you don't want it to melt).
3. Roll mixture into tight, 1-inch balls and place in the freezer for 15 minutes to set.

Chocolate Mousse

(Serves 4)

After a delicious meal (of chickpeas), we all need something sweet to tell our stomachs the meal is done, right? Something that strikes the right balance between light and decadent. Well look no further! You can choose your own adventure by adding one of the optional toppings.

Ingredients

¾ cup dark chocolate or chocolate chips, roughly chopped
1 cup aquafaba
¼ tsp cream of tartar
½ tsp vanilla extract

Optional toppings

Chickpea Caramel Sauce (page 136)
Pomegranate with Dark Chocolate Chunks
Aquafaba Coconut Whip (page 137) with Fresh Raspberries

Directions

1. Slowly melt chocolate in a bowl placed over a pan of simmering water. Set aside to cool completely.

2. Combine aquafaba and cream of tartar. Using electric beaters or a stand mixer, mix liquid for 10 to 15 minutes until stiff peaks form (you should be able to tip the bowl upside down with contents staying put), and then add the vanilla.

3. Slowly fold the chocolate into the aquafaba mixture and gently stir to ensure chocolate is incorporated with no lumps. Note: If making the Aquafaba Coconut Whip, reserve 1 cup of aquafaba before adding the chocolate. The aquafaba will reduce slightly once chocolate is added, but don't be alarmed.

4. Transfer into small serving bowls and place in fridge for at least 30 minutes.

5. Remove from fridge and top with one of three optional toppings.

Chickpea Caramel Sauce

(Yields 1 cup)

You read that right: There are chickpeas blended into this sauce. This way you never need to think "should I put caramel sauce on this?" because the answer is yes. Yes, you should.

Ingredients

1 cup full-fat canned coconut milk, room temperature

¾ cup coconut sugar or brown sugar

¼ cup chickpeas cooked or canned

¼ tsp coarse sea salt

Directions

1. Place all ingredients in the blender, and blend until smooth

2. Pour mixture into pot over high heat and bring to a boil.

3. Reduce to medium-low medium heat and simmer for about 15 minutes, until caramel has thickened, stirring occasionally. It should be sticking to the back of your spatula or spoon.

4. Remove pan from heat. Allow to cool slightly for 10 minutes then transfer to an 8-ounce mason jar with a lid. Place in fridge to thicken for at least 2 hours.

5. To use, simply remove from fridge and pour over anything you want.

Aquafaba Coconut Whip

(Yields 1 cup)

Aquafaba can act like whipped cream, and in this version, the toasted coconut and maple syrup give it beautiful sweetness and texture. The perfect accompaniment to the mousse, or pie, or anything you'd like whipped cream on.

Ingredients

1 cup whipped aquafaba
2 tbsp shredded coconut, toasted
1 tbsp maple syrup
3–4 raspberries per serving

Directions

1. Reserve 1 cup of aquafaba before chocolate is added to the mousse.

2. Toast coconut over medium-high heat in skillet for 2 to 3 minutes, stirring frequently, until browned.

3. Fold the maple syrup into the whipped aquafaba and add toasted coconut, dollop on mousse, and add raspberries.

Rice CrisPEA Squares

(Makes 9 squares)

This is a delicious, easy-to-make snack to keep yourself—or little ones—going. Plus, it's nut-free so you can bring them places nuts are not welcomed. Add a chocolate drizzle and you have a fancy treat without all the sugar.

Ingredients

¼ cup dark chocolate chips
¼ cup cooked or canned chickpeas, mashed
¼ cup tahini
½ brown rice syrup
¼ tsp salt
1 tsp vanilla
3 cups puffed rice cereal
¼ cup sunflower seeds
¼ cup pepitas
⅛ cup hemp hearts
¼ cup chopped dates or apricots

Directions

1. Slowly melt chocolate in a bowl placed in a pan of simmering water. Set aside to cool.
2. In a large pot over low heat, add mashed chickpeas, tahini, and brown rice syrup, and stir until softened and well combined.
3. Remove from heat and stir in salt and vanilla.
4. Fold in puffed rice cereal, sunflower seeds, pepitas, hemp hearts, and chopped fruit.
5. Pour into an oiled 8 x 8-inch pan and press firmly.
6. Add melted chocolate to a pastry bag (or sandwich bag with the corner cut off) and let your inner chocolate artist loose.
7. Cover pan with plastic wrap and chill in the refrigerator for 30 minutes.

Peanut Butter Chocolate Chunk Cookies

(Makes 1 dozen cookies)

These chewy cookies have all the goodness of the classic peanut butter and chocolate combo and you could practically pass them off as protein bars. The good news is you won't be tempted to eat the batter (chickpea flour isn't tasty before it's cooked), which means you get to eat an extra cookie!

Ingredients

1 cup chickpea flour
½ cup almond flour
¾ cup coconut sugar
½ tsp baking soda
½ tsp salt
3 tbsp coconut oil, melted
¼ cup applesauce
1 tsp apple cider vinegar
1 tsp vanilla
½ cup peanut butter
½ cup of 70% cacao chocolate, chopped

Directions

1. Preheat oven to 350°F.
2. In a large bowl, combine the chickpea flour, almond flour, coconut sugar, baking soda, and salt.
3. In another bowl, combine coconut oil, applesauce, apple cider vinegar, vanilla, and peanut butter.
4. Mix together the wet and dry ingredients (this is best done with your hands). Add the chocolate and form into 2-inch balls (wetting your hands while rolling the balls will help the dough not stick to your hands).
5. Place onto an oiled cookie sheet about 2 inches apart. Bake for 15 minutes until golden brown.

New Zealand Pavlova

(Serves 8–10)

Heather was fortunate enough to marry into a family of Kiwis. One of her favorite desserts before she became vegan was pavlova. The real deal is full of eggs, so we were determined to find a vegan version of this masterpiece. Enter aquafaba—the miracle liquid that's found in every can of chickpeas (or reserved from the beans that you cook). When whipped for long enough, it turns into what resembles whipped cream. This stunning desert can be served on its own or with fresh seasonal berries and some additional icing sugar.

Ingredients

1 cup aquafaba
¼ tsp cream of tartar
¾ cup granulated sugar
½ tsp vanilla
2 cups mixed fresh berries
(e.g., blueberries,
raspberries, blackberries,
strawberries)
2 tbsp icing sugar

Directions

1. Preheat oven to 200°F.
2. Combine aquafaba and cream of tartar.
3. Using electric beaters or a stand mixer, mix liquid for 10 to 15 minutes until stiff peaks form. Throughout this process, slowly add the sugar, 1 tablespoon at a time.
4. Once stiff peaks form (you should be able to tip the bowl upside down with contents staying put), add the vanilla.
5. Set aside 1½ cups of the whipped aquafaba.
6. Place large dollops of the remaining mixture onto a large parchment-lined baking sheet, about 1 to 2 inches apart.
7. Bake for 2 hours, turning the sheet halfway through. Turn the oven off and let sit in the hot oven for 1 more hour.
8. Remove from oven, carefully transfer to a tray, and top with uncooked whipped aquafaba, berries, and icing sugar, if desired.

Dark Chocolate Bark with Chickpeas, Hazelnuts & Sea Salt

(Serves 4)

Hazelnuts are like the long-lost sister of the chickpea, don't you think? They look so similar and once you smother them with dark chocolate, it becomes impossible to tell them apart! When you bite into this bark, you never know what you're going to get. But you come out a winner either way. If you can stop yourself from eating the whole batch, this bark makes for beautiful gifts around the holidays. Hazelnuts also go by the alias of filberts, but don't be fooled by the silly name. Apologies if your name is Filbert.

Ingredients

1½ cups cooked or canned chickpeas
1 tbsp coconut oil
½ cup roasted hazelnuts
1 cup dark vegan chocolate chips
½ tsp sea salt

Directions

1. Preheat oven to 450°F.
2. Rinse chickpeas then gently rub dry with a clean kitchen towel. Allow to air dry until dry to the touch.
3. Place them in a medium bowl, coat with coconut oil, and cook for 25 minutes, shaking tray halfway through to rotate beans. After 25 minutes, turn off oven and leave the beans in the warm oven for another 10 minutes.
4. Place hazelnuts on a baking tray and roast for about 10 minutes, until golden brown, shaking the pan occasionally. Remove from oven and set aside.
5. Meanwhile, place chocolate in a heatproof bowl and put in a pot of gently simmering water. Allow chocolate to slowly melt, stirring often.
6. Once melted, add roasted chickpeas and hazelnuts to the bowl and coat completely with chocolate. Spread onto a parchment-lined baking sheet, ensuring all the chickpeas and hazelnuts are flat. Sprinkle with sea salt.
7. Place tray in fridge and cool until the chocolate is solid, about 30 minutes. Cut or break into pieces.

Double Chocolate Chickpea Cupcakes

(Makes 2 dozen cupcakes)

One of our favorite Toronto bakeries, Yummy Stuff, has a knack for vegan cupcakes. We were thrilled when they agreed to develop a chickpea version of their masterpiece for our book. This cupcake will blow your mind with its chocolatey goodness. And the fact that it's made with chickpea flour means it's helping you reach your protein goals for the day. And your delicious goals. This recipe makes a lot of cupcakes, so you'll either be the star of a party, or you'll have a lot leftover. Good news is they freeze really well, so you can revisit Chocolate Heaven any time you wish.

Ingredients

For the cupcakes

2 cups chickpea flour
1⅔ cups granulated sugar
1 cup cocoa
2 tsp baking soda
1 tsp baking powder
¼ tsp salt
1¾ cups soy milk
2 tsp red wine vinegar
1¼ cups canola oil
2 tbsp vanilla

For the frosting

2 cups vegan margarine (room
    temperature)
2½ cups icing sugar
1 tbsp vanilla
10 oz bittersweet chocolate,
    melted & cooled to room
    temperature
¼ cup soy milk

Directions

For the cupcakes

1. Preheat oven to 350°F.
2. Combine flour, sugar, cocoa, baking soda, baking powder, and salt.
3. Whisk together wet ingredients, pour into flour mixture, and stir until combined.
4. Scoop into muffin tins lined with paper cupcake liners. Bake for approximately 25 minutes, until toothpick comes out clean. Allow to cool.

For the frosting

1. Using electric beaters, combine margarine and icing sugar, beat on low for about a minute.
2. Add vanilla and chocolate, and beat on medium speed until smooth. Add milk and beat for an additional minute.
3. Spread on cupcakes and serve.

Chocolate Chickpea Brownies

(Makes about 9 brownies)

These simple brownies are so rich and satisfying, you'll only need one . . . or maybe two. They're also incredibly healthy, so you needn't feel guilty if you do eat the whole batch! They're high in protein and fiber and low in sugar and saturated fat. These are not as durable as traditional brownies (in other words, they're crumbly), so try to serve when warm right out of the oven and don't attempt to pack them on a seven-day trek in the mountains.

Ingredients

1½ cups cooked or canned chickpeas
½ cup cocoa powder
¼ cup organic brown sugar
¼ cup coconut oil
¼ cup soy milk
1 tsp vanilla extract
½ tsp baking powder
¼ tsp salt
¼ cup vegan chocolate chips

Directions

1. Preheat oven to 350°F and lightly oil an 8 x 8-inch baking pan (or similar size).

2. In a food processor, add chickpeas, cocoa powder, sugar, oil, soy milk, vanilla, baking powder, and salt. Pulse until well combined (scraping down sides as necessary).

3. Spread mixture into pan. Top with chocolate chips and bake for 22 to 24 minutes.

4. Remove from oven and transfer to a cooling rack, allowing to cool before cutting into squares.

Berry Tart

(Serves 6–8)

Although chickpeas can be found in all components of this dish, the star of this dessert is the whip on top. You'll be blown away by how simple it is to make a fluffy vegan whip cream—with only two ingredients. Tip: If you don't have a spring form pan, place strips of parchment paper under the crust for easy lifting.

Ingredients

¼ cup softened coconut oil, plus more for brushing pan
2 cups almond flour
½ cup chickpeas, canned or cooked, divided
1¼ cup medjool dates
½ tsp sea salt
¼ cup almond butter
¼ cup maple syrup or agave
1 tsp brown sugar
¼ cup aquafaba
⅛ cup granulated sugar
3 cups mixed berries (e.g., raspberries, sliced strawberries, blackberries, or blueberries)
1 tbsp icing sugar

Directions

1. Brush a 9-inch spring form pan with softened coconut oil.

2. Make dough by placing almond flour into a food processor, along with ¼ cup chickpeas, dates, and salt and combine until a dough forms.

3. Press dough into the spring form pan to form a crust. Put pan in the freezer for 10 minutes.

4. In a high-speed blender or food processor, add almond butter, remaining ¼ cup chickpeas, coconut oil, maple syrup or agave, and brown sugar and process until smooth. Remove tart from freezer and pour on top. Place in fridge for 10 more minutes.

5. Meanwhile, pour aquafaba into a large mixing bowl. Using electric beaters or a stand mixer, mix liquid for 10 to 15 minutes until stiff peaks form (you should be able to tip the bowl upside down without contents falling out). Throughout this process, slowly add ⅛ cup sugar, 1 tablespoon at a time.

6. Spread whip evenly on tart, top with mixed berries, and sprinkle with icing sugar.

Chapter 8
Tips, Hacks & Libations

Chickpea "Tofu"

(Makes approximately 4 cups)

This versatile "tofu" can be used in anything from stir-fry to sandwiches or soup. It can be made into french fries (see Triple Threat Poutine on page 41 and Chickpea Fries with Sage Dip, page 34), baked in the oven to make polenta-style crackers (page 20), or used to replace soy-based tofu in Teriyaki Chickpea Tofu (page 112). It's straight forward to make but requires some of time. So, if you're planning on adding it to a dinner recipe, start prepping the evening before. Note: You will need cheesecloth on hand to line your loaf pan. It will absorb water and help you remove it from the pan.

Ingredients

1¼ cups chickpea flour
4 cups water
½ tsp olive oil
½ tsp sea salt
¼ tsp turmeric
¼ tsp garlic powder

Directions

1. In a medium bowl, add chickpea flour and water. Allow to sit for 2 hours.

2. Over medium to low heat, warm olive oil in a pot and carefully pour in the liquid from the bowl without disrupting the goopy mixture at the bottom.

3. Add the salt, tumeric, and garlic powder and whisk well to combine. Simmer on low for 10 minutes, stirring frequently until the mixture thickens.

4. Once liquid becomes thicker, add the goopy mixture from the bottom of the bowl. This will thicken things considerably. Whisk constantly for about 10 minutes.

5. Line a loaf pan with cheesecloth and pour mixture into the pan and smooth with a spoon. Let cool on the counter, then refrigerate until firm, at least two hours, or overnight. Once set, flip onto a cutting board and tofu should slip out. Remove cloth. Slice according to your recipe requirements.

The Perfect Batter

(Makes about 1½ cups of batter)

At University, we used to go to our student pub for a platter of "Deep Fried." Important to note here is that it didn't really matter *what* was being deep fried, only that it was crispy, salty, and awesome. This no-fail vegan substitution will serve for all of your indulgent frying needs. It's quick and easy to whip up and easy to double (or triple) if you're entertaining a crowd. We get into all kinds of trouble with this recipe—using it on just about everything from veggies to tofu. For an extra crispy addition, have a bowl of panko or breadcrumbs on hand. Dip the lucky veggie into the batter first, then the panko, and then the oil for frying. Devine!

Ingredients

1 cup chickpea flour
1 tsp garlic powder
1 tsp fine sea salt
1 tsp onion powder
1 cup almond milk

Directions

1. Mix dry ingredients together then slowly whisk in almond milk until well combined and all lumps are removed.

The Perfect Roasted Chickpea

Roasting the perfect bean is a great trick to have up your sleeve and will come in handy for snacking. See Roasted Chickpeas (A Few Ways) on page 35, or page 37 to create a spicy crunchy topping for all your spicy crunchy topping needs. They're also used in a delectable Chickpea Parmesan on page 159. The recipe below starts you off on the right foot for your own culinary creations.

Ingredients

1½ cups cooked or canned chickpeas
2 tbsp olive oil

Directions

1. Preheat oven to 450°F.
2. Rinse chickpeas then gently rub dry with a clean kitchen towel. Allow to air dry until dry to the touch.
3. Coat with olive oil and cook for 25 minutes, shaking halfway through to rotate beans. Turn off oven and leave the beans in the warm oven for another 10 minutes.

Cooking Dried Chickpeas

(Makes 5 cups of cooked beans and 1 cup aquafaba)

Canned chickpeas aren't very expensive but working with dried beans is a fraction of the price. You also reduce the packing and have the chance to make homemade aquafaba. As many of our recipes call for about 1 can of chickpeas, consider freezing them in small containers with about 1½ or 2 cups, which is about what's found in 15- to 19-ounce cans. See how organized you are?

Ingredients

2 cups dried chickpeas
8 cups water

Directions

1. Place chickpeas in a large pot or bowl and cover completely with water. As they absorb the water, you may need to add additional water once or twice. Allow to sit overnight or for about 12 hours.

2. Drain, rinse, and place in a pot with 8 cups of fresh water. Bring to a boil.

3. Reduce heat and allow to simmer with lid on for about 90 minutes (darker chickpeas may require up to 30 additional minutes). They should be tender but not mushy. If making aquafaba, remove beans and continue to simmer the cooking water until it's the consistency of egg whites. Otherwise, drain and rinse (some of the skins will have fallen off) and allow to cool. They're now ready to go!

Chickpea Mayonnaise

(Makes about 1 cup)

While vegan mayonnaise is becoming more readily available in supermarkets, sometimes it's nice to have a from-scratch option for special occasions. You can use it on sandwiches, in dips, and it's also great for our Chickpea Fries with Roasted Sage Dip (page 34). We like to store it in an 8-ounce mason jar for easy access. Note: This recipe calls for an electric hand mixer, but also works well if using a stand mixer (in which case, you may find that the mayo is ready sooner than the 10 to 12 minutes called for below).

Ingredients

¼ cup aquafaba
1½ tbsp fresh lemon juice
1 tbsp agave syrup
1½ tsp apple cider vinegar
⅛ tsp cream of tartar
⅛ tsp ground mustard
½ tsp sea salt
¾ cup canola oil

Directions

1. In a large mixing bowl, combine all ingredients except oil. Using an electric hand mixer, begin to mix while very slowly adding canola oil over a period of 5 minutes.
2. Continue mixing for an additional about 10 to 12 minutes until mixture is thick and creamy.

Marinated Chickpeas

(Makes enough to fill an 8-oz jar)

This recipe was adapted from a kalamata olive marinade famous among our friends. Turns out chickpeas are happy to drink up this delicious mixture, which transforms them into incredible flavor balls that will kick your salad up a notch. They're also perfect to eat on their own in an appetizer spread or during a snack attack.

Ingredients

¾ cup cooked or canned
    chickpeas
¼ cup olive oil
3 tbsp balsamic vinegar
2 cloves garlic
Juice from ½ lemon
3 springs fresh thyme

Direction

Add all ingredients to an 8-ounce mason jar, shake well, and store in the fridge. These chickpeas will be tasty after a few days and will last for about 2 weeks.

Chickpea Parmesan

(Makes about 1 cup)

The extra crispy roasted chickpeas in this recipe offer high nutritional value with a superb cheesy flavor. You'll love the flavor of this parm, and it's an excellent fridge staple to keep on hand to sprinkle on pasta or soup or just eat by the spoonful from the jar.

Ingredients

½ cup chickpeas, cooked or canned
1 tsp olive oil
1 cup unsalted almonds
4 tbsp nutritional yeast
1 tsp sea salt
1 tsp garlic powder

Directions

1. Preheat oven to 450°F.
2. Rinse chickpeas then gently rub dry with a clean kitchen towel. Allow to air dry until dry to the touch. Don't worry about removing the skins; this will make the chickpeas even crunchier.
3. Coat with olive oil and cook for 30 minutes, shaking the tray halfway through to rotate beans. After, turn off oven and leave the beans in the warm oven for another 10 minutes. You want these suckers to be super crispy! Then allow to cool.
4. Combine all ingredients in blender or food processor until you have a crumb-like texture. Do not over-blend.
5. Store in the fridge in an airtight container.

Chickpea Bread

(Makes 6–8 thick slices)

Hot out of the oven bread is heaven sent. This protein-packed version is no exception, with its crispy crust and soft center. It's perfect for sandwiches, to serve alongside soup, or just on its own with butter. It needs to sit for 18 to 24 hours, but it's worth your pre-planning efforts. If you intend to serve for dinner, throw the ingredients together the afternoon of the day before.

Ingredients

1 cup chickpeas, cooked or canned
1⅓ cup water, divided
2¾ cups all-purpose flour, plus more for dusting
¼ cup chickpea flour
½ tsp yeast
1 tsp sea salt

Directions

1. Place chickpeas and ⅓ cup water in a high-speed blender or food processor and process until smooth.

2. Combine flours, yeast, and salt in a large bowl and add chickpea mixture plus remaining 1 cup water. Stir until well combined (dough will be well mixed but lumpy and sticky). Cover tightly with plastic wrap and set it aside to rest at room temperature for 18 to 24 hours.

3. When dough is bubbly, place it on a floured surface and roll over on itself a few times. Place dough on a well-floured tea towel and top with additional flour. Let sit for an additional 1 to 2 hours.

4. Place a ceramic dish with a lid on the middle rack of the oven and preheat the oven to 450°F. Using oven mitts, remove the ceramic dish from the oven and remove the lid. Pick up the dough by sliding your hand under the towel and flipping it over into the dish. Again, using oven mitts, give the dish a small shake to even out the dough (it will continue to take shape when baking).

5. Return lid to dish and bake bread for 30 minutes covered. Remove lid and continue to bake for 12 to 15 minutes, or until bread is golden brown. Allow to cool and enjoy!

Pickled Chickpeas

(Makes enough to fill a 32-oz mason jar)

A more than distant cousin to the humble jalapeño, chickpeas are not to be overlooked when it comes to pickling! They're perfect on top of soups or salads, tucked in tacos, or on a skewer in your Caesar (page 170). Feel free to double (or triple) the recipe. They also make unique gifts—nothing says "Happy Holidays" or "I'm glad you were born" like a jar of pickled chickpeas.

Ingredients

1 cup white wine vinegar
1 cup water
1 tbsp coarse sea salt
1 tsp coriander seeds
1 tsp black peppercorns
4 large jalapeños, thinly sliced
3 cups chickpeas, cooked or
    canned
1 bay leaf
1 garlic clove, thinly sliced

Directions

1. Combine the vinegar, water, salt, coriander seeds, and peppercorns in a small saucepan over high heat, bring to a boil, and turn off the heat.

2. To an empty mason jar, add jalapeños, chickpeas, bay leaf, and garlic slices.

3. Once cooled, pour the vinegar mixture over the jalapeños and chickpeas (it should cover them completely).

4. Check that the lid is tightly screwed on and (perhaps standing over the sink) tip the jar upside down to ensure the spices and garlic are evenly distributed.

5. The chickpeas will be pickled and tasty after a few days and will last for about 2 weeks.

Homemade Aquafaba

(Makes 1 cup aquafaba and 5 cups of cooked beans)

If you're ready to graduate from using canned aquafaba to making your own, the pioneers would be proud of you. Some swear that homemade is superior to the canned liquid, and we agree: homemade aquafaba is thicker and creamier than the canned version. It might seem like a daunting task, but if you're cooking dried beans anyway, you might as well save the cooking liquid and get the bragging rights from making it from scratch.

Ingredients

2 cups dried chickpeas
8 cups water

Directions

1. Place chickpeas in a large pot or bowl and cover completely with water. As they begin to absorb the water, you may need to add additional water once or twice. Allow to sit overnight or for about 12 hours.

2. Discard water, rinse beans, and place in a pot with 8 cups of fresh water. Bring to a boil.

3. Reduce heat and allow to simmer with the lid on for 90 minutes.

4. Turn off the heat and leave chickpeas to cool in the pot, uncovered, allowing more of the protein that will result in the foam to infuse the cooking water.

5. Remove the cooked beans with a clean slotted spoon (grease is the enemy of aquafaba).

6. Simmer for another 30 minutes with the lid removed to reduce liquid further until it's the consistency of egg whites. You will be left with a yellowish viscous liquid. Voila, aquafaba!

Sprout Your Own Chickpeas

It's hard to believe but you can make the chickpea even more nutritious and digestible by sprouting the dried beans. Plus, it's surprisingly easy to do yourself with just a few simple supplies and a little forethought. Toss these nutrient-dense bundles on your salads and feel like you're winning at life.

Ingredients and Equipment Needed

A large glass mason jar
Cheese cloth
Canning jar ring
½ cup dried chickpeas

Directions

1. Rinse dried chickpeas and place in a large mason jar.

2. Fill the jar with water and use the cheesecloth with the canning ring as the lid. Allow the beans to soak for 24 hours.

3. Drain and rinse the beans through the cloth, and repeat. Leave the drained jar on its side out of direct sunlight at room temperature. Repeat every 8 to 12 hours. After about a day, little sprouts will become visible from the tips of the beans. Allow the sprouts to grow the length you desire: ¾ inch is usually good. This will take around 2 to 3 days in total.

4. Once sprouted to the desired length, rinse and drain them once more and allow sprouted chickpeas to air dry.

5. Store in an airtight container in the fridge.

Lavender Whiskey Sour

(Makes 1 cocktail)

Aquafaba cocktails are becoming all the rage in bars around the globe. Aquafaba provides a wonderful froth and texture, and we promise you won't miss the raw egg white that's typically used . . . because, yuck. This Whiskey Sour recipe is sweet, tangy, and just as frothy as the real thing. We infused a bottle of Jameson with 4 to 5 lavender sprigs the night before to create a subtle floral aroma and taste.

Ingredients

2 oz Jameson Whiskey
¾ oz aquafaba
¾ oz simple syrup
Ice cubes
Sprig of fresh lavender, for serving

Directions

1. Place whiskey, aquafaba, and syrup in a cocktail mixer or mason jar. Shake for about 20 seconds.
2. Place ice in a glass, pour drink on top, and garnish with sprig of lavender.

Chickpea Caesar

(Makes 1 cocktail)

Canadians love their Caesars! A Caesar is the Northern version of a Bloody Mary, but with clam juice added to the tomato juice. For those who get a bit squeamish with the thought of drinking clams, this vegan version is for you! The best part about creating a Caesar is that you can play around with the garnish. In the spirit of celebrating the chickpea, we've used our Pickled Chickpeas (page 163) to make this drink pop. Bottoms up!

Ingredients

1 tsp lemon juice
⅛ tsp coarse sea salt
⅛ tsp celery salt
⅛ tsp fresh ground pepper
Ice cubes
1½ oz vodka
A dash of tabasco
A dash of vegan
   Worcestershire sauce
1 cup vegan Caesar Mix (we
   like Simp's Serious Caesar
   Mix) or tomato juice
3 tbsp pickled chickpeas
Other garnishes, if desired
   (e.g., pickled string beans,
   asparagus, olives, or celery.)

Directions

1. Place lemon juice in a small flat dish. Combine salt, celery salt, and fresh ground pepper into another dish. Dip glass, upside down, in lemon juice and then in salt mixture to create a rim around the edge of the glass.

2. Add desired amount of ice, followed by vodka, tabasco, Worcestershire sauce, and Caesar mix or tomato juice. Stir well.

3. Place chickpeas on a toothpick or skewer. Place on top of drink and serve. Enjoy!

Spicy Margarita

(makes 1 cocktail)

Jen and her husband fell in love with this drink on their honeymoon, and they have been making it ever since. It is the perfect cocktail to sip on a hot day. The trick is to marinate serrano peppers in the tequila. If that feels like too big a commitment, then decant some tequila into a smaller bottle and marinate in there (be sure to overestimate, one will not be enough!). In this version, aquafaba is used to create a beautiful foamy top so that lime zest enjoys a prominent spot on the drink and won't sink to the bottom like a loser.

Ingredients

1½ oz tequila, that has had serrano peppers marinating for a day or more, depending on your spiciness desires

¾ oz triple sec liqueur

1 oz fresh lime juice

¾ oz aquafaba

Lime wedge for side of the drink

Salt for the rim

Lime zest for garnish

Directions

1. Slice serrano pepper in half so that it can fit into the bottle of tequila. Let marinate for one day, or longer if you're a spice lover.

2. In a cocktail shaker (or mason jar), combine tequila, triple sec, lime juice, and aquafaba and shake vigorously for 20 seconds.

3. Prepare a glass by rubbing a lime around the rim and dipping it into a plate of salt. Add lime wedge to edge of glass.

4. Fill the glass with ice (this is important, as the ice stops the aquafaba from foaming), pour drink, and garnish with lime zest.

Pisco Sour

This sweet-and-sour cocktail originated in Peru, and the main ingredient—Pisco—used to be difficult to come by. Lucky for us, it's becoming more readily available in North America. A classic Pisco Sour has a frothy egg white topping. In our recipe, aquafaba takes over, creating a similar foamy finish.

Ingredients

⅓ oz aquafaba
1 oz lemon juice
1½ oz Pisco
⅔ oz simple syrup
Lime slices, for serving

Directions

1. Add all ingredients to a cocktail shaker (or mason jar) and shake vigorously for 20 seconds.
2. Add ice cubes to a glass, pour drink on top, and garnish with a slice of lime.

Endnotes

1 "Goal 13: Take urgent action to combat climate change and its impacts." *Un.org/ Sustainabledevelopment*, United Nations, www.un.org/sustainabledevelopment/climate-change-2/.

2 Pierson, Jimmy, et al. "Why animal agriculture's environmental impact is still being ignored." *Environment Journal*, 6 June 2016, environmentjournal.online/articles/animal-agricultures-environmental-impact-still-ignored/.

3 "Goal 13: Take urgent action to combat climate change and its impacts." *Un.org/ Sustainabledevelopment*, United Nations, www.un.org/sustainabledevelopment/climate-change-2/.

4 Stehfest, Elke, et al. "Climate benefits of changing diet." *SpringerLink*, Springer Netherlands, 4 Feb. 2009, link.springer.com/article/10.1007/s10584-008-9534-6. https://link.springer.com/article/10.1007%2Fs10584-008-9534-6

5 *Livestocks long shadow: environmental issues and options*. Livestock, Environment and Development Initiative, Food and Agriculture Organization of the United Nations, 2006, ftp://ftp.fao.org/docrep/fao/010/a0701e/a0701e.pdf. ftp://ftp.fao.org/docrep/fao/010/a0701e/a0701e.pdf

6 Wellesley, Laura, and Antony Froggatt. "Changing Climate, Changing Diets: Pathways to Lower Meat Consumption." *Chatham House*, 24 Nov. 2015, www.chathamhouse .org/publication/changing-climate-changing-diets.

7 "Soil Improvements With Legumes." *Government of Saskatchewan*, Agriculture Knowledge Centre, www.saskatchewan.ca/business/agriculture-natural-resources-and-industry/agribusiness-farmers-and-ranchers/crops-and-irrigation/soils-fertility-and-nutrients/soil-improvements-with-legume

8 "Food and climate change." *David Suzuki Foundation*, www.davidsuzuki.org/what-you-can-do/food-and-our-planet/food-and-climate-change/?q=print

9 Hiroko Tabuchi, Claire Rigby And Jeremy White. "Amazon Deforestation, Once Tamed, Comes Roaring Back." *The New York Times*, The New York Times, 24 Feb. 2017, www. nytimes.com/2017/02/24/business/energy-environment/deforestation-brazil-bolivia-south-america.html.

10 Solomon, Susan, et al. *Climate Change 2007: The Physical Science Basis—IPCC*. Cambridge University Press/Intergovernmental Panel on Climate Change , www.ipcc. ch/report/ar4/wg1/.

11 *Chickpea.* The International Crops Research Institute for the Semi-Arid Tropics, http://exploreit.icrisat.org/profile/Chickpea/232

12 Ibid.

13 "Climate Resilient Chickpea Innovation Lab | Agrilinks." *Feed the Future Innovation Lab for Climate Resilient Chickpea*, U.S. Government's Global Hunger and Food Security Initiative, https://agrilinks.org/activity/climate-resilient-chickpea-innovation-lab.

14 Pierson, Jimmy, et al. "Why animal agriculture's environmental impact is still being ignored." *Environment Journal*, 6 June 2016, environmentjournal.online/articles/animal-agricultures-environmental-impact-still-ignored/.

15 *Chickpea.* The International Crops Research Institute for the Semi-Arid Tropics, http://exploreit.icrisat.org/profile/Chickpea/232

16 "Chickpea." *CGIAR*, Consultative Group on International Agricultural Research, www.cgiar.org/our-strategy/crop-factsheets/chickpea/.

17 Wellesley, Laura, and Antony Froggatt. "Changing Climate, Changing Diets: Pathways to Lower Meat Consumption." *Chatham House*, 24 Nov. 2015, www.chathamhouse.org/publication/changing-climate-changing-diets.

18 Moore, Heather. "Make America great: Follow Canada's expected diet recommendations." *TheSpec.com*, TheSpec.com, 28 July 2017, www.thespec.com/opinion-story/7476649-make-america-great-follow-canada-s-expected-diet-recommendations/.

19 M.S.L.J. *Why eating more vegetables is good for the environment.* The Economist , 16 Apr. 2016, 19. http://www.economist.com/blogs/economist-explains/2016/04/economist-explains-12.

20 Ibid.

Acknowledgments

Enormous thanks to:

- Our team of terrific testers: Jenny Ball, Jojo Chambers, Mike Hollenbeck, Tania Howells, Dana Lloyd, Caity Mulqueen, Merrilyn Mulqueen, Rebecca Sproat, Julia Trau, Nancy van Keerbergen
- To all those who came camera-ready to dine on chickpeas late into the night: Dana, Joanna, Jenny, Rebecca, Caity, Erin, Sean, Sabrina, Robin, Mike & Mike
- Our brilliant photographer, Josh, for loving chickpeas as much as we do and for always knowing when something was "flat" and how to fix it
- Andy and Debbie, for providing a beautiful space to work and set up giant lights
- Mima, Pops, Grandma & GrandMark, for all your wrangling allowing for the time needed to make this happen
- The Mulloskeys for your love of vegetables, Erin for starting the veg roast tradition, and Evan, for having the cutest, chubbiest hands
- Sabrina, for being our favorite artist
- James, for sharing your chana skills
- Mary Anne, for all your pretty things
- Wendy, for her extensive therapy and eagle-eyed editing
- Morag from Yummy Stuff, for developing the Best. Cupcake. Ever.
- Olivia, for getting your dad to "spill the beans" on his secret marinade
- Eileen & Marc, for the fresh chickpea delivery
- Our editors, Nicole Frail and Emily Shields, for believing in our book concept and helping us navigate the world of publishing
- The extensive and tireless work of researchers, advocates, and activists who help to make the planet more sustainable and compassionate

Conversion Charts

METRIC AND IMPERIAL CONVERSIONS
(These conversions are rounded for convenience)

Ingredient	Cups/Tablespoons/Teaspoons	Ounces	Grams/Milliliters
Butter	1 cup/16 tablespoons/2 sticks	8 ounces	230 grams
Cheese, shredded	1 cup	4 ounces	110 grams
Cream cheese	1 tablespoon	0.5 ounce	14.5 grams
Cornstarch	1 tablespoon	0.3 ounce	8 grams
Flour, all-purpose	1 cup/1 tablespoon	4.5 ounces/0.3 ounce	125 grams/8 grams
Flour, whole wheat	1 cup	4 ounces	120 grams
Fruit, dried	1 cup	4 ounces	120 grams
Fruits or veggies, chopped	1 cup	5 to 7 ounces	145 to 200 grams
Fruits or veggies, puréed	1 cup	8.5 ounces	245 grams
Honey, maple syrup, or corn syrup	1 tablespoon	0.75 ounce	20 grams
Liquids: cream, milk, water, or juice	1 cup	8 fluid ounces	240 milliliters
Oats	1 cup	5.5 ounces	150 grams
Salt	1 teaspoon	0.2 ounces	6 grams
Spices: cinnamon, cloves, ginger, or nutmeg (ground)	1 teaspoon	0.2 ounce	5 milliliters
Sugar, brown, firmly packed	1 cup	7 ounces	200 grams
Sugar, white	1 cup/1 tablespoon	7 ounces/0.5 ounce	200 grams/12.5 grams
Vanilla extract	1 teaspoon	0.2 ounce	4 grams

OVEN TEMPERATURES

Fahrenheit	Celsius	Gas Mark
225°	110°	¼
250°	120°	½
275°	140°	1
300°	150°	2
325°	160°	3
350°	180°	4
375°	190°	5
400°	200°	6
425°	220°	7
450°	230°	8

Index

About the Authors

Heather Lawless (a.k.a. The Lawless Vegan) is a blogger and freelance writer. She's worked for nonprofit organizations around the globe and has advocated for women's equality as a consultant with the United Nations Development Fund for Women. She currently works for the provincial government in the area of income support policy and lives in Scarborough, Canada, with her husband and kids.

Jen Mulqueen is a certified culinary nutrition expert who believes in the power of food to nourish and create a better world. Her background is in documentary production, and she now works with Roots of Empathy to help create more emotionally literate and empathic children. She resides in Toronto, Ontario, Canada, with her husband and two children.